THE ELECTRICIAN'S BOOK OF Trade Secrets

ATLAS PUBLISHING
Hauppauge, NY

The
Electrician's
Book of
Trade
Secrets

Copyright © 2007 W Marketing, Inc. All rights reserved.
Printed in the United States of America. Except as a protected under the United States of America Copyright Act of 1976, no part of this publication may be reproduced or distributed in any form or by any means, or stored in a data base or retrieval system, without the prior written consent of the publisher.

ISBN 1 94 6798851

For special quantity discounts on this and other technical titles, contact Atlas Publishing at:

30 Oser Avenue, Suite 500
Hauppauge, NY 11788
1.888.226.7052
www.atlaspublishing.com

The information contained in this book has been obtained by the publisher from sources believed to be reliable. Atlas Publishing, the authors, printers or agents make no guarantee of the accuracy or completeness of any information published herein and neither Atlas Publishing or its authors shall be responsible for any errors, omissions, or damages resulting out of the use of this information. It should be understood that Atlas Publishing and the authors are offering information but are not attempting to render comprehensive or complete information on which this book is based.

TABLE OF CONTENTS

Introduction 4
The Number One Trade Secret 6
How To Use a Regular AC Motor As A Generator 9
A Convenient Method for Bending PVC Conduit 16
An Easy Method of Temporary Fusing 16
Customizing Trouble Lights 17
A Device That Can Automatically Balance a Panel 19
Removing Blockages In Conduit 20
Running An Underground Circuit Without Hurting The Sod 22
Using Worn Cadweld Molds 23
Bobby's Method of Fishing The Impossible 23
How To Remove Type S Fuse Adaptors 25
Getting Three Phase Power From Single Phase 26
Insulation Guard For Recessed Fixtures 27
Phantom Voltage 28
Home Made Ground Rod Driver 30
Prefabbing 31
A Unique Way To Trim A Panel 32
Fishing EMT Through Bar Joists 35
Getting A Third Hand 35
The Art of Slabbing 36
Wiring Through A Roof-Top Unit 37
Patching Holes in Walls 38
Using A Conduit Bender As A Vise 39
Combining A Time Clock & A Photo-cell 40
Getting A Good Ground In Poor Soil 42
The Old-Time Flatters 42
A Cable Dish 44
Using Stilts To Install Cable 45
Sectional Bag For Fittings 46
The Best Work Apron 47
Greasing Motor Bearings While The Motor Is Running 48
Running A Three Phase Motor On Single Phase Power 48
Using A Bare Grounding Conductor 51
Installing EMT Above A Suspended Ceiling 52
Using a 2x2 Floor For A High Frequency Ground 53
Using Templates 55
Expansion Joints 56
Running Power Tools From Your Automobile Alternator 56
Using A Ladder As A Work Station 60
Analyzing The Leads Of A Nine Lead Motor 62
Miscellanious Tricks 66
Roughing in a Building for Different Voltage Systems 67
Mobile Temporary Power Centers 70
Tapping Into Trade Magazines 71
Miscellanious Thoughts On Fishing Wire 73
Fishing The Impossible 77
Credits 79

Table of Contents

THE NUMBER ONE TRADE SECRET

What is the number one trade secret? Understanding what it takes to be a first class electrician.

What is it that makes someone a top electrician? Well, we break it down into three separate characteristics:
1. The pursuit of excellence
2. A concern for safety
3. An understanding of why things work, not just how they work

You know, years ago the term " Electrician" referred to a very professional vocation. In recent years, the term has gotten cheap. There are lot of people who are called an electrician who are miles away from being what we call a "Real Electrician".

To give you an idea of how the meaning of the term has changed down through the years, we'll share something with you that we ran across recently: Around the turn of the century there was a man named Telsa who actually invented AC motors as we know them today. Further, he was the man who made the discoveries that led to the development of the radio. He gave lectures to the London Institution of Electrical Engineers, etc. Here's the point; in his own day he was called "One of the nation's top electricians." At that time the term "Electrician" carried some esteem; not so anymore'.

Now we'll go through these three characteristics one by one and explain a little better what it is that makes a "Real Electrician."

THE PURSUIT OF EXCELLENCE

What is the pursuit of excellence? Very simply put: it is wanting to be good at what you do. A man who pursues excellence doesn't want to be mediocre, or do "good enough." A real electrician wants to be good at what he does. That doesn't mean that he is trying to be better than other people, but that he just wants to be good at what he does. Not for someone else's sake, but for himself.

It doesn't take a genius to be a Real Electrician; but it does take effort. It takes a person who cares enough to spend a little more time than they "have to"; it takes a little more study; a little more thought; a little more concern. Most people are quite capable of attaining excellence, but very few do. To achieve excellence, a person's driving force must be internal, not just external.

A CONCERN FOR SAFETY

Have you ever worked with an old-time electrician and asked him to do something that was questionable, as to whether it was safe or not? If you ever have, you probably remember that he didn't do it. Why? Because he's been around long enough to know what electricity incorrectly used can do. He has seen it first hand, and he knows that as an electrician it is his responsibility to make sure that it doesn't happen.

As unpleasant as it is, think about this: How, would you feel if a house that you wired had an electricral fire and several people died? It wouldn't feel very good, would it? This isn't a far out story, it has happened before hundreds of times--maybe thousands. The old-timer has seen it before; he remembers who the electrician who did the bad wiring was; he remembers where the house was; he may even remember the names of the people who got killed. The old-timer knows that electricity can be dangerous; he has seen for himself what it can do.

Some of the most deadly fires that have ever been were started by electricity. This is why the electrical code had to be written; that is what keeps Underwriter's Laboratories in business; if electricity is not used properly, it can be deadly.

Here is one thing to remember: Even with codes, inspectors, U. L. labels, and everything else that regulates the industry; in the end, the responsibility for safety lies with the person who installed the wiring. Why did they install something in someone's building that wasn't safe? Maybe they say that they didn't know it wasn't safe. Well, that's certainly better than doing it purposely, but why did the person go ahead and install it in someone's house if they didn't know enough to tell if it was safe or not?

Safety is the electrician's responsibility. Unfortunately, many of the younger electricians don't really understand just how dangerous electricity can be; they think that the faster they can slap up their work the better. Hopefully they will realize their responsibility to the people who live and work in the buildings they wire before disaster strikes.

UNDERSTANDING WHY THINGS WORK NOT JUST HOW THEY WORK

This, is what separates the men from the boys as far as we are concerned. A real electrician knows why things work. To illustrate the point, here is a conversation that we heard several years ago:

A group of several electricians (some of them 20 year veterans) were standing together 'in one part of an electrical contractor's shop. They were discussing motors. Here is an approximate transcript of how the conversation went:

Electrician A: OK Joe, how do you reverse a single phase motor? (Joe mutters something and waits, hoping that someone else will answer the question.)
Electrician B: I know how, you reverse number 4 and number 7.
Electrician A: Are you sure?
Electrician B: Yeah, I did it twice last month. (At this time, up walks the estimator; the only real electrician of the bunch.)
Electrician A: Hey Howard (the estimator), how do you reverse a single phase motor?
Estimator: What you have to do is to reverse the start winding.
Electrician B: What?
Estimator: You reverse the start winding. When you do, you are reversing its polarity, and the motor's magnetic field will rotate the opposite direction.
Electrician B: You're crazy, you have to reverse 4 and 7; that's how you do it..

Do you see the difference in these men's attitudes? (This is a true story by the way.) All Electrician B cares about is what number wires he has to change; he doesn't at all care why it works. Actually, he passed off the estimator as silly for talking about polarity and the rotation of the magnetic field.

The estimator was concerned with what makes the machine work; he could hardly care less what number the wires are.

So what is the difference? The estimator can reverse the motor, but so can Electrician B.

Here's the difference: The estimator knows what makes that motor turn, he can fix any single phase motor anywhere in the world. If the motor is a different voltage, that's fine; if its wires aren't numbered, that's fine too; if the motor won't operate properly, he can figure out why; if he wants the motor to do something a little bit different, he can figure out how to do that too.

Electrician B can do none of this, he only knows how to twist wire nuts on wire number 4 and wire number 7; beyond that he is lost.

Here is the core of the issue: When you know what makes things work, you can make changes in them; you can figure out why they aren't working properly if that be the case; in short, you can do anything you want to with that machine. The estimator is a professional that can deal with almost anything; Electrician B might as well be on the assembly line screwing part Y to part Z.

To us, a Real Electrician knows why a motor turns; he understands why a transformer works; he understands magnetic theory; he knows why the over-current protection for different types of equipment can have different settings; the list goes on and on. If you don't know why things work, you are merely following "connect A to B" type directions. When you do know why things work, you become a professional.

Sadly, Real Electricians are hard to find; and the reason for this is that most electricians really don't care enough. Hopefully that will change.

How To Use A Regular AC Motor As A Generator

HOW TO USE A REGULAR A.C. MOTOR AS A GENERATOR

Almost any A.C. motor will work as a generator. Here's how it works for a standard "squirrel cage" motor:

First of all, you will need something to drive the motor with (this is also called the "prime mover"), what the source is doesn't really matter, as long as it is fairly consistent in speed. A small gasoline engine which drives the motor with a belt usually works quite well.

If you can drive the motor (properly called an "Induction Generator" when used this way) at 4-5% faster than synchronous speed, you will get almost exactly 60 cycle power. The frequency depends on how fast you turn the motor/generator. For a standard single phase motor with a synchronous speed of 1800 rpm (synchronous speed is the

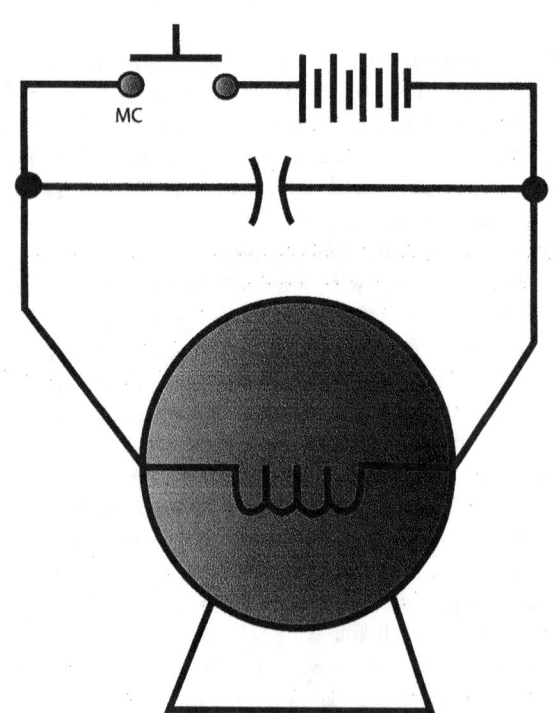

Single phase induction generator

speed of the rotating magnetic field; the actual speed at which the shaft turns is a little slower, in this case about 1725 rpm) you would have to turn the shaft at about 1880 rpm to get 60 Hz power.

Because AC motors have a rotating magnetic field, they don't usually retain any concentrated magnetic field (called residual magnetism); because of this, a motor used as a generator this way often won't start producing electricity by itself. Fortunately, this is pretty easy to take care of.

If you look at the sketch above, you will see that we are showing a battery and momentary contact switch in parallel with the motor.

We use this battery power to give the motor a little jolt which will get it started generating power. All we need to do is to get a small current started in the windings and the motor/generator will take over on its own. We use this momentary contact switch to give it power for just an instant; a standard start switch would be perfect. What type of batteries you use doesn't really matter, as long as the voltage is enough to get a little current started in the windings. Usually 12 volts will do, although sometimes you may need more. An auto battery will usually do very well. (As a note: If you need more voltage, you can just hook up another battery in series with the one you are already using; when you connect batteries in series, their voltage is additive. For example: A 12 volt battery and a 6 volt battery connected in series will produce 18 volts.)

You will also notice from this drawing that we are showing a capacitor, which is also in parallel with the motor/generator. As noted in the drawing, this is optional. If you are using a split-phase, capacitor run type of motor, you will not need this capacitor. For other types of split phase motors however, you should use a capacitor as is shown here. Depending on the type and characteristics of the motor you use. this capacitor should be anywhere from 9 to 100 mfd (microfarads). You will have to test each motor/generator individually to see what works best. Be careful though, that the capacitor you use is rated for the voltage you want to use it on; for motors, always try to go higher than the operating voltage, as motors can generate some unusually high voltages when they start and stop. A capacitor rated 250 volts or more should work fine. Also make sure you use what is called an AC capacitor (which is really two capacitors connected back to back), an electrolytic type is usually the cheapest and best.

On page 12, we are showing the same type of set-up, but this time for a three phase motor. You notice that the connections are almost exactly the same. The only real difference between the two types of motors is that using a single phase motor will give you single phase, 120 volt power, and the three phase motor will give you three phase, 240 volt power (or 208 volt, depending on the type of motor). Whatever voltage the motor is wound for will be the type of voltage you get from it.

Don't expect to get as much power out of this generator as the motor nameplate states. Due to the losses in the generator, the generator output is less. If you overload the generator, the output current will abruptly cease. This is characteristic of an induction generator that can be unpleasant, but really is a great benefit, as the motor/generator cannot burn out, which would be far worse.

Every now and then you will run into a motor that because of its internal design characteristics will not work this way properly. The number of motors that don't work well is very few, however.

For some loads to operate well (particularly motor loads) you will need your power output to be very close to 60 cycles (also called Hertz, or Hz). Here's an easy way to calibrate the frequency of your power: Take a regular electric clock (motor driven type, which is the typical variety), and connect it to, the power output of your motor/ generator.

Check the time of the electric: clock against a quartz wristwatch (or any type of watch; we say quartz because it is a little more accurate); and then adjust the speed at which the shaft of the motor is driven until the electric clock and the wristwatch are in unison. Because these electric clocks are made to keep accurate time based on 60 cycles, they will run faster or slower if the frequency of the power feeding them is faster or slower than 60 Hz.

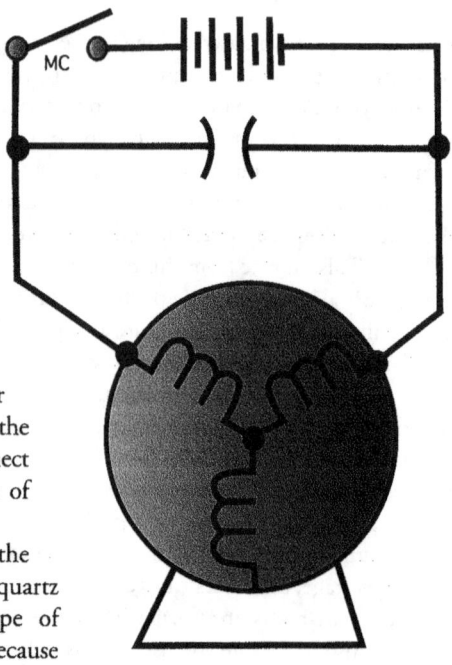

Three phase induction generator

THEORY OF OPERATION

Since the rotor of a squirrel-cage motor has no wires in it, and no electricity fed to it, just how it can be used to generate power is a mystery to many electricians. Here is a description of exactly how and why it works:

Let's start by going through the way this machine works as a motor, and then go from there.

When the machine is connected to a source of AC power, it produces a magnetic field that rotates around its stator windings. The speed at which this field rotates around the stator is called synchronous speed. This speed is equal to 120 times the frequency of the current, divided by the number of poles in the motor. For a standard single phase motor this would be 120 times 60 Hz (which equals 7,200) divided by four; which comes to 1,800. This means that the synchronous speed of the motor is 1,800 rpm.

This rotating magnetic field produces magnetic flux (think of magnetic flux as waves of magnetism) that crosses the air gap between the stator and the rotor. This flux then moves across the bars of the squirrel-cage rotor, and induces a current to flow through these rotor bars. This is the same principal that makes a transformer work; any time a magnetic field passes through a conductor, it creates a current in the conductor. (This is called inducing a current in the conductor.)

So now we have a current in the bars of the rotor; here's what happens: Because there is a current flowing in the bars of the rotor, there will also be a magnetic field set-up around the rotor bars. (Any time there is a current flowing in any conductor, there will be a magnetic field that forms around it. Current flow creates a magnetic field; this is a basic characteristic of electricity and magnetism.)

So what happens, is that the magnetic fields of the rotor and stator attract; and since the stator's magnetic field is moving at synchronous speed, it tends to pull the rotor with it. This is what makes the rotor turn.

There is one more factor that comes into play here; it is called the motor's "slip". If you have ever noticed, an average single phase motor has a speed of about 1725 rpm. A few paragraphs back, we explained that the magnetic field that rotates around the stator moves at 1,800 rpm. The difference between the synchronous speed and the speed at which the motor's shaft actually turns is called the amount of slip. In this case, the amount of slip is 4-5%, which is typical.

All squirrel-cage motors will have a certain amount of slip; if they didn't, they couldn't operate. If the speed of the stator's field and the speed of the rotor's field were equal, the stator's magnetic field would not cut across the rotor bars, as they would stay even with each other at all times. There would be no relative motion between the two, and the rotor would get no current induced into it, and therefore would have no magnetic field set up around it. The amount of slip depends mostly upon how much of a load the motor is trying to turn. The harder the load is to turn--the more slip there will be; the easier the load is to turn--the less slip there will be.

So now that we've explained the machine's operation as a motor, let's get into its operation as a generator.

We start off with no current flow in either the rotor or the stator; the machine is doing nothing. Let's say that we connect a 100 watt light bulb to the leads from the motor (which is now being used as a generator). Now we start to turn the shaft of the motor/generator. What happens now? Nothing. (Unless there is some residual [left over] magnetism in the motor / generator.) There is no current flow in either the rotor or the stator; therefore there can be no magnetic field, and no movement current generated.

So now we give the stator windings a quick shot of DC current, as we said before. Now what happens? The DC current flows through the stator windings, setting up a magnetic field around these windings. This small magnetic force crosses over the air gap, and cuts across the rotor bars, just like it did for motor operation.

Now, the rotor (which is being forcefully turned) begins to move around the stator, taking its magnetic field with it. This magnetic field now cuts across another section of the stator, and induces a current into it. Now the light bulb lights up, the machine is operating as a generator.

The brief shot of DC current is enough to get a current started in the stator. After these first steps take place (in a fraction of a second) the rotor will get the magnetism that induces the current in its rotor bars from the current which it generates. Because it is being forced along, the rotor forces the magnetic field along.

In generator operation, just as in motor operation, there is a certain amount of slip. So if you want your generator to put out 60 cycle power, you will have to turn the shaft at about 4-5% more than synchronous speed. This is exactly the opposite of how the motor worked.

There are, of course, more things that could be said about magnetic theory, counter EMF, and other fine points; but this is a good general explanation of how the machine operates. Go through this explanation slowly, and try to picture each step. Once you start to get an understanding of how electricity, magnetism, and mechanical force work together it is a fascinating subject.

USING A CONDUCTION GENERATOR FOR COGENERATION

Here is a very interesting fact about the induction generators that we have been talking about:

If you hook them up to a regular AC power and drive them above their synchronous speed, they will generate power with the same voltage and frequency as the AC line. The faster beyond synchronous speed that you drive them, the more power they will put out (within limits).

When you drive the induction generator (which is the same thing as an induction motor as you recall) without any outside voltage source, the frequency of the power is puts out depends upon the speed at which you drive the machine. But in this case, you are feeding a certain type of current (60 cycle) to the machine before you start to generate power. Until you drive the machine faster than synchronous speed it will be (and act like) a motor. However, once you pass synchronous speed, the machine will start putting out power. This power will have the same characteristics as the current that has already set up the machine's magnetic field.

The great advantage of this, is that you can tie an induction generator that is run this way directly into the AC system. You do not need to take any other steps to make sure the power that your generator puts out is compatible with the rest of the system, as you do with other types of generators. The generator is inherently self-regulating; whatever the power on the AC line is like, that's what kind of current the induction generator will put out.

This makes any type of extra or wasted power usable. (This is usually limited to factories, as individual stores or homes don't put out enough wasted power to make it reasonable to put out the money to construct a cogeneration system.) As long as there is more than enough power available to drive the machine faster than synchronous speed, you can probably save money by generating some of your own power this way.

A CHEAP AND CONVENIENT METHOD FOR BENDING PVC CONDUIT

As most electricians know, bending PVC conduit is not very difficult; provided the conduit has first been properly heated.

There are a number of methods currently in use for the heating of PVC conduit, all of which require some type of tool or appliance. This creates two problems: First of all, that some of these benders are fairly expensive; and secondly, that they are not always on the job when you need them.

Here is one easy solution:

Take the piece of conduit that you need heated, and slide it over the exhaust pipe on your work truck. Use some duct tape to seal the openings (for smaller sizes of conduit use a fair amount of duct tape, as they aren't large enough to slip over the exhaust pipe), and let the truck idle for ten minutes.

This usually does a very fine job of heating the conduit, without over-heating it. When properly heated, the conduit should be pliable, but not completely limp.

If you ever get brown or black spots in the conduit. it has been heated too much. throw that piece away and start over.

As always, take care when you bend the pipe to avoid putting any kinks in it. Be careful that the exhaust fumes (which will be coming out of the conduit now. rather than out of the exhaust pipe) will be a sufficient distance away from anyone else working the area.

For some of the larger sizes of conduit a little more time may be required to properly heat the conduit.

EASY, TEMPORARY FUSING

We knew an electrical contractor who did a lot of emergency type work (fire jobs and the like). Often this contractor's men had to come into damaged buildings, and make quick repairs under adverse conditions.

Here is an idea that one old-time electrician came up with that is a real help in tough circumstances:

Many times this man had to restore power to a burned out building for clean-up and removal operations. When he got to the power panels, he usually found nothing in usable condition except the main disconnect. So, it being that he had to get temporary power hooked up as quickly as possible; and that connecting a branch circuit to a main disconnect (usually fused at no less than 200 amps, and often higher) is quite dangerous; he did this:

Take a regular temporary lampholder (also called a pigtail socket; the kind that is used for temporary lighting), and instead of screwing a bulb into it, screw in a plug fuse (use an "S" type). Then you can connect one side to the power source, and the other end to the branch circuit; as shown on page 18.

You should also put a couple of wraps of tape around the lampholder's leads so the wires don't pull apart. As always, make sure everything is properly supported and protected.

Here's one more note: If you have a need for more current, take two or three lampholder/fuse assemblies, and hook them up in parallel. However, if you do this, make sure you make good, solid connections.

Remember, this is for temporary use only; if you need power for an extended period, you should install a permanent wiring system. You can refer to Article 527 for the 2002 NEC or Article 590 for the 2005 NEC for further requirements regarding temporary electrical installations.

CUSTOMIZING TROUBLE LIGHTS

Almost all electricians are familiar with the use of trouble lights (also called "drop-cord lights"). Those electricians who do a lot of service work and trouble calls would be especially familiar.

Here are a couple of ideas on customizing your trouble lights that will make your job a little easier:

If you take a fairly strong magnet, and glue it onto the side of your trouble light, you will find that finding somewhere to stick it up will be much easier; anything made of iron or steel will do. This can really be handy. Refer to the drawing on page 19 where this is shown.

Make sure that you use a good grade of epoxy glue, so it will hold tight for a number of years.

Here's another:

We heard about one guy who took an old trouble light, and cut off the plug, stripped back the cable sheath and insulation on the ends of

Customizing Trouble Lights

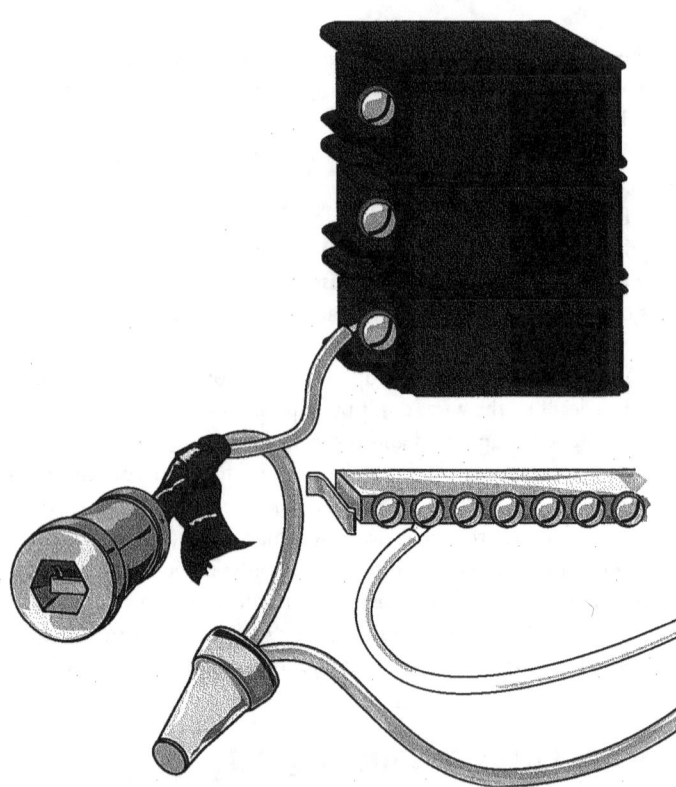

Temporary fusing arrangement

the wires, and then put alligator clips on the ends of the wires. (See illustration on page 20.)

Then he went out and got a 12 volt light bulb, and put it into the trouble light instead of the 120 volt bulb.

What this man did was to keep this trouble light in the back of his truck, so if he were to have any problems with it, or if he wanted to do some work on it in the evening, all he had to do was to slip the alligator clips onto the vehicle's battery terminals.

We think that having a trouble light set up is almost a must as a safety item. We would have thought that someone would be selling these commercially, but we don't recall ever seeing them.

You can get 12 volt light bulbs from almost any electric supply house; if they don't have them in stock, they should be able to order them without any trouble.

For whatever types of trouble lights you use, we recommend that you use "vibration service" bulbs. They cost more than regular bulbs, but last far longer. The big reason for using these bulbs however, is that when you drop them, their filament almost never breaks. There are not too many situations that are worse for a serviceman than dropping his trouble light in a tight attic, and finding himself in complete darkness.

If you can't find vibration service bulbs, the "rough service" bulbs and the "tough-skin" bulbs do well too.

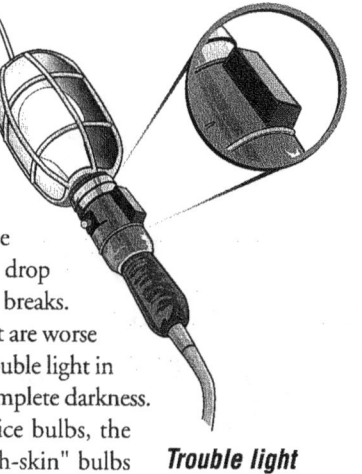

Trouble light with magnet

A DEVICE TO AUTOMATICALLY BALANCE A PANEL

As most electricians know, a power panel that has voltage imbalances between phases can cause some real problems. These imbalances can cause motors to burn out quickly, and are damaging to many other types of equipment also.

Not long ago we ran across a unique type of electronic device that can automatically balance a circuit breaker panel (or any other type of panel also).

The device is marketed as a transient surge suppressor but it has a unique type of bridging circuit that is used to dissipate large amounts of power. What this does is to transfer some current from one phase to another.

When wired into a power panel, the device will route imbalance power from one phase to another (at the appropriate point in the other phase's cycle of course), thus balancing the panel. Besides this, it's also the best transient surge suppressor that we've ever seen.

The company that makes this device doesn't market it for balancing panels; their expertise is in sensitive electronics, and they aren't too famil-

12 volt trouble light

iar with power circuitry. Never the less, we've seen the test reports, and we are convinced. (It balanced 19 panels at a Ford Motor Co. factory; which we consider pretty impressive).

The device is fairly expensive (about $600.00 for a 277/488V, 3 phase, 4W unit), but is a breeze to install. It mounts in a 1/2" knock-out, and is wired either to the lugs or a circuit breaker.

The device itself is nothing more than a cast aluminum box (a Bell box) with the electronic components inside, sealed in epoxy so no one can find out how it works.

Doing some quick hunting online should yield several sources or you could contact your local electrical supply house for some help in locating this type of unit.

REMOVING BLOCKAGES IN CONDUIT

Getting a conduit blocked with concrete (or anything else for that matter) can be a major problem. This usually happens to underground runs when someone accidentally spills some foreign substance into an open conduit. Probably the most common blockage is drywall joint compound, which is fortunately not too hard to break up. Concrete, however, can be a major problem. Most other blockages are the result of "dirty tricks", such as nails dropped into the conduit.

The first answer obviously, is to keep all of your conduits well capped. This means covering them up as soon as they are in place; even if you leave them uncovered for just one day, there's no telling that it won't be the day that someone makes a mistake.

The first step once you find that you have a blockage in the run is to use your fish tape and try to get through the blockage by pushing and twisting the fish tape. Work with it for a while and try to break through. If the blockage is drywall joint compound, you can often get through it this way. If this doesn't get you through, then your problem is probably concrete. The easiest way we know of to deal with concrete in your conduit is this:

Take a wound type of fish tape (rather than the spring steel type; originally called a "Sparks" tape), and cut off the end. Then, weld or braze a small masonry drill bit onto this end. Be careful to keep the bit and tape lined up together, as if you don't you will have a lot of wobble as you drill. Then push the fish tape into the conduit until the drill bit contacts the blockage. Put the other end of the tape into a drill, and start drilling through the concrete. This is a tough process, but you really have no good choice.

Removing Blockages In Conduit

There is one other method we know of, but we don't recommend it to anyone but a demolition expert:

We heard a few years back about some electricians who ran into a problem with concrete in their pipes. They worked on the blockage, but had no success. Well, it happened that one of the electricians had been a demolition expert when he was in the military. This fellow somehow got a hold of a blasting cap. He then set everything up (we don't know the details of this) and detonated it, removing the blockage completely. Remember that this guy was an expert who had done this type of thing many, many times before. He knew how to set it up; and how big a charge he could use, and still not blow a hole in the conduit. They also had to make sure that the area around the blast, and on both ends of the conduit were clear, so that no one would end up getting hurt.

When you have to deal with a blockage in a conduit, take some time to think the whole thing over before you start hammering away. How far into the pipe is the blockage? Exactly where does that put the blockage? (under what part of the building, etc.). Can you get the fish tape through from the other side? Is there a pull box or other fitting that you are running into, rather than concrete? These questions are kind of elementary, but you might be surprised how often people don't use common sense.

Blockages of concrete and drywall joint compound usually occur at the first 90 degree elbow, or at the end of the run. If the blockage is in the middle of the run, it is probably something else. Find the exact location of the blockage, and try to determine what in that area may have caused the conduit to be blocked. Blockages in the middle of a long run are pretty hard to deal with; if they are outdoors, you will probably have to dig up the pipe; if the blockage is under part of the building, you may not be able to do anything but start over.

HOW TO RUN AN UNDERGROUND CIRCUIT THROUGH A WELL MANICURED YARD WITHOUT DISTURBING THE SOD

Running An Underground Circuit Without Hurting The Sod

We got this idea from an electrician who specialized in custom residential work. He did a lot of work for well-to-do customers.

These customers had him do quite a bit of outdoor lighting and the like; but they were very concerned about him tearing up their yards in the process.

So here's what he did:

He would get a flat spade (the flatter the better), push it straight into the ground, and they wobble it back and forth to cleave the ground. Then he pulled the spade back out, and did the same thing all the way across the yard. Of course when he got to the other end, he laid his cable in this little crevice.

Then to close up the trench, he would walk the length of the trench with one foot on the side of the trench, and one foot on the other. If you can do this and walk with very small steps, you can push the sod back together just like it was before.

This method is a little bit slow, but when you are done, you can't tell at all that you ever opened a ditch there.

When you do this, take care to get the cable buried deep enough (Code requires a minimum depth of 12 inches for GFCI protected residential circuits up to 20 amps, 120 volts).

USING WORN CADWELD MOLDS

CADWELD type graphite molds will usually wear out after 50 uses or so. Because of the incredible amount of heat that the exothermic welding process creates, after a number of uses the graphite will wear away at the points where it gets the most friction and pressure.

The problem with this is not really the expense of buying a new mold, but the time that is usually necessary to get one. Often it can take weeks to get a certain type of mold. Obviously this can cause problems.

If you ever find yourself in a problem like this, this is what you can do:

Take some ductseal (the kind that is used to seal underground conduits as they enter a building) and fill the voids in the mold with it before you ignite the charge.

The ductseal is heat resistant enough that it will usually survive the welding process.

The best way to do this is to spread a thin coat of the ductseal on all the surfaces of mold that must seal. If there are any parts of the mold that have been chipped off, fill in these areas before you close the mold.

Be careful to keep the ductseal out of the crucible area (the part of the mold where the molten metal will be); if you were to get the ductseal mixed in with the molten metal, you could affect the quality of the weld.

Using Worn Cadweld Molds

One other note: If you ever run out of the little metal disks for the bottom of the mold-use a penny, it works just fine.

BOBBY'S METHOD OF FISHING THE IMPOSSIBLE

This is one of the most interesting stories about fishing wire into an almost impossible location that we've ever heard. Here is the story (we've verified this with eye witnesses, by the way):

There was a school in Bobby's area that needed to get a number of circuits run from one part of the building to another; so they called Bobby's boss, who was one of the top electrical contractors in the area. As it happened, Bobby's company got the job, and sent Bobby out to get it done. Well, the first of the circuits went fine, but one day they realized that they were going to have a problem getting another one of the circuits in: The ceilings were plastered (this was before suspended ceilings were used very widely), and there was only about a six inch space between the ceiling and the bottom of the roof steel. To make things worse, the length of the run was about two hundred feet.

So the electrical contractor called the people from the school board, and asked them to come down to the school so he could show them the problem, and explain why it was impossible for him to get the circuit in. So the next day the people from the school board meet the contractor on the job, and get an explanation of why it just can't be done. Well, in the middle of this explanation Bobby walks up and says "Don't worry about it boss, I've got it all figured out; it won't be any problem." The boss answers: "Bobby, there's no way under the sun that you can get that circuit in there, it's impossible." But Bobby replies that he knows he can do it; so they all agree to give him a chance at it.

So the next morning Bobby walks into the school with a fan in one hand; and in the other hand a paper bag and an extension cord. By this time, the other electricians had dropped what they were doing, and were waiting to see what Bobby had up his sleeve.

The first thing Bobby does is to set up the fan above an access panel at one end of the proposed run. Then he pulls a can and a canopener out of his paper bag; he opens the can and puts it in front of the fan. (By this time all the other electricians are really wondering what this guy is up to).

One more thing: he goes out to the truck and comes back carrying a cat; he ties a string around the cat's collar, and puts the cat into the ceiling void through another access panel on the other side of the run from the fan. It turns out that the can Bobby opened was catnip; and, of course, the fan blows the smell towards the cat, who goes right to it. Then Bobby takes a leisurely walk over to the other end of the run (by the fan), reaches up and pulls the cat back down (with the catnip, of course). They tie their cable to the string that had been tied to the cat's collar, and pull it in.

The wire's in; the school board saves a bunch of money; and Bobby is Electrician of The Year. True story.

Bobby's Method of Fishing The Impossible

HOW TO REMOVE A TYPE "S" FUSE ADAPTOR FROM A FUSE HOLDER

Most electricians are familiar with the use of type "S" fuse adaptors, also called "fuse-stat" adaptors. These adaptors fit into a regular fuseholder (the same as a medium base on a light bulb; also called Edison base) and will only accept a certain type of plug fuse. These adaptors coordinate with different sizes of fuses (size meaning ampacity) so that a certain adaptor will only accept a fuse with a certain ampacity rating. This has been done to eliminate the problems that arose when someone would pull a fuse out of an overloaded circuit and replace it with a larger fuse. This larger fuse often had a higher ampacity rating than the branch circuit wiring that it supplied. Because of this there have been numerous fires and lost lives.

While the type "S" adaptors work very well, they do cause some problems for electricians. The most difficult problem is in trying to replace or change one of these adaptors. Since they are designed to be tamper-proof, they can be rather difficult to work with.

How To Remove Type S Fuse Adaptors

We knew one electrician who did a lot of work in older buildings where he ran into a lot of these adaptors that needed to be changed; here is his method of removing them:

First is to cut off power to the fuse panel.

Next, make several cuts in the outer lip of the adaptor. Then peel back each of these sections carefully. You will need to do a pretty good job of getting them bent all the way back.

Once you get these sections bent back, you will see the wire inside of the adaptor that keeps the adaptor in place. You will need a good pair of needle-nose pliers; get a good grip on the wire, and twist it out (this is kind of like unwindlng it from the adaptor). Once this is done. you can just unscrew the adaptor as you would any fuse.

GETTING THREE PHASE POWER FROM SINGLE PHASE

Here is the easiest way we know to get good three phase power from a single phase; it has some limitations, but overall, it works very well.

To start with, you will need a standard three phase induction motor (Delta wound is preferable to Star) and a capacitor (an electrolytic type is usually alright, as it won't really be carrying the load current; it is needed for power factor correction).

As you see in the accompanying schematic on page 27, you bring both legs of your single phase power to two leads of the three phase motor, and continue them into the three phase power system; the third leg of the three phase system will come from the last lead of the motor, as shown in the schematic.

Your power factor capacitor will be connected between the motor lead which is not connected to one of the single phase legs and to the continuing portion of one of the single phase leads (see drawing for clarification). The best value of a capacitor to use is usually somewhere between ten and twenty-five mfd (micro-farad), but this value is not critical. You can start with a ten mfd capacitor, and then add additional capacitors in parallel until you get no more improvement in performance.

The three phase motor will start by itself once power is connected to it if you use the proper value of capacitance. If it doesn't, you can switch some' additional capacitors into the circuit momentarily. If you really have trouble getting the three phase motor started, you can use a small single phase motor with a belt drive to bring the three phase motor up to speed.

The typical load that is usually run on a system like this is three phase motors, here are a couple of things to remember about using three phase motors on this type of system:

- You can usually start a motor up to the same horsepower rating as the motor you are using to convert the single phase power to three phase, but not larger.
- You can usually power a total load four times larger than the rating of your converter motor. For example: if the motor you are using to convert the single phase power to three phase is 10 horsepower, you should be able to run 40 horsepower of load on the system.

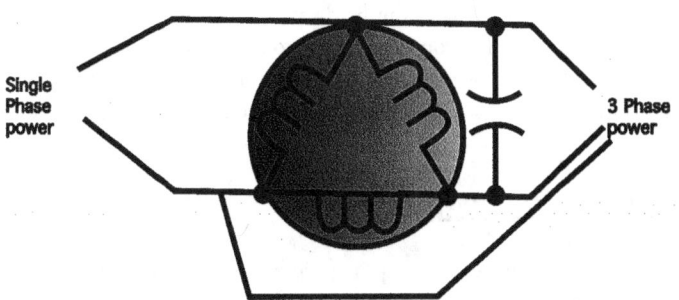

Set-up for generating three phase power from single phase

Because of the difficulty of getting balanced current in all phases, you should not run motors at more than 80% of their rated load on this system; if you did, you would run the risk of overheating any motors on this system. Starting torque for the first motor run on the system is usually not too good (about 60%), but if you add more motors, this figure will improve significantly.

Remember that the voltage rating of your three phase motor should match the voltage of your single phase power.

A CHEAP AND EASY INSULATION GUARD FOR RECESSED LIGHT FIXTURES

When installing recessed light fixtures, it is required that the fixtures have a minimum 3 inch clearance of any thermal insulation (except if they are approved for the purpose) to prevent overheating. (NEC Section 410.66(B).) Besides being required, we consider this to be trade practice.

Here is the easiest way we know of to do this:

Take a piece of what is called "Hardware Cloth." This is a type of wire mesh fencing that people use for keeping rabbits out of their gardens, etc. Depending on what type of insulation you will be working with, you will want to use a larger or smaller size of hardware cloth (the hardware cloth comes in various sizes of mesh: 2" x 2", 4" x 4", etc.). For very fine blown-in insulation, you may need to cover the hardware cloth with screening material before the insulation is installed.

What you do is to take the hardware cloth, and bend it to shape around the fixture. Then you can fasten it to either the fixture itself, or to the ceiling framing by using push nuts. Push nuts are the little sheet metal pieces that you can push over a wire or rod to hold something in place.

PHANTOM VOLTAGE

Phantom voltage can be a quite perplexing problem to electricians. So, while phantom voltage isn't a trade secret, we feel that having a good understanding of what it is and how it works is well worth explaining.

Phantom voltages are voltages that occur typically in systems with long runs of insulated wire in metallic conduit. These voltages are caused by capacitance between the wires and the conduit; or sometimes between one wire and another wire in the same conduit. These voltages can produce some pretty odd results.

The first time we ever encountered phantom voltage we were a little taken back by it; here's what happened:

Phantom Voltage

One afternoon a call came in from an electrician who was wiring a large discount store nearby. He said "Can you get down here right away? I've got some crazy voltages; something is wrong." Not only was this electrician embarrassed about messing up the job, but he was quite concerned about someone getting hurt.

So we went to the site – the store was almost complete, and the store's people were already setting up shelves; the power was on, the lights were lit, everything looked OK. We went to the back of the store and found the panels; sure enough, the voltages were crazy, we had never seen anything quite like it.

The service to the building was a 480/277 volts, three phase, four wire, wye system. The 480/277 volt system fed all of the lighting and HVAC units. There were three separate stepdown transformers throughout the building to bring the voltage down to 208/120 for receptacles, etc.

We checked the 480/277 volt panels, which seemed fine. Then we went to the 208/120 panels: Phase A to ground: 120 volts. Phase B to ground: 0 volts! "See what I mean," says the electrician, "something is wrong". We had to agree. Phase C to ground 120 volts. Phase A to phase B: 208 volts. Phase A to phase C: 208 volts. Phase B to phase C: 120 volts! Next, we check neutral to ground: 120 volts!

26

At first we thought there might have been something wrong with one of the step-down transformers; but after we checked all of the transformer's internal connections we pretty well ruled that out. Then we came up with the answer. We asked the electrician: "Is the system bonded?" "Yeah," he says, "All the transformers have their bonding jumper hooked up, and they all are connected to ground rods." "What about the 480 volt system," we asked. "I'm not positive" he says; "I'll send someone to check." "But that wouldn't make any difference," he said: "The 480 volt system is fine, it's the low voltage system that's got problems. " We had the man check anyways.

So, the man went and checked, and found that the bonding jumper in the main 480 disconnect hadn't been hooked up yet. Then he installed the jumper, and we had them go back and check the voltages again: thankfully everything was back to normal. "Why did the jumper on the 480 volt disconnect make a difference to B phase in the 120 volt system?" asked the electrician. We really didn't have an answer to give him except that we knew a lot of crazy things happen with open bonds or open neutrals.

Eventually we got an answer from the people at Sorgel transformer. They explained that it was a phenomenon called phantom voltage, and that it is usually the result of poor ground connections. They asked if the building had any long runs of insulated wire in metal pipe; we said that there were several feeders from one end of the store to the other, which was about 200 feet. They said that they were sure the problem started there, as a capacitive voltage between the conductors and the metal conduit. They said that this voltage will show up on a volt meter, but the actual current that it can generate is usually so small that it poses no great danger (except to computers).

Why did a capacitance in a 480 volt feeder affect B phase on a 120 volt system? No one knows. We have to go back to what we learned as a first year apprentice: "Weird things happen when you open a neutral, or don't bond the system properly."

If you ever run into what you think might be a phantom voltage, the first thing to do is to check your grounding connections, and your bonds. In the case of this discount store, the conduit system didn't have a good path for the ground current. There were quite a few driven ground rods used to ground the conduit system; but this capacitive voltage could not find a good path back to the main transformer which fed the system; this was because the soil in the area was very sandy (hence a very high resistance), and the transformer was a pretty fair distance away. Once the bonding jumper was hooked up however, the capacitive voltage was drained off the system through the neutral, which now was solidly connected to both the transformer and the conduit system.

Improving your grounding and/or bonding system is almost always the answer for phantom voltage problems. In the few instances where there are problems between individual line conductors, the only good answer we know of is to go to a shielded transformer. However, we recommend that you have an electrical engineer look at your problem before you go to that expense.

A HOME MADE GROUND ROD DRIVER

You can make an excellent ground rod driver from must a few dollars worth of materials. Here's how:

Take a piece of 1-1/4 inch rigid steel conduit about 4 feet long. Remove any sharp edges. Then get a piece of steel that weighs 30 to 40 pounds and weld it onto one end of the 1-1/4 inch pipe. Try to get a piece of steel that is fairly compact (cylindrical would be perfect) and flat on the side that is going to be welded to the pipe. After you are done with your welding, you should give the whole thing a good coat of rust resistant primer followed by a very tough grade of paint.

The way to use this is to slide the driver over the top of the ground rod, then lift it and drop it on the rod to drive it into the ground. The 30 plus pounds of steel falling repetitively on the ground rod does a fine job of driving it in almost any type of soil. See the illustration at right for clarity.

Ground rod Driver

PREFABBING

If you are doing a job with a lot of recessed light fixtures, you can save a lot of time by prefabbing your ceiling junction boxes.

The typical way to do this is to first make up all of your fixture whips. (You can use 3/8 inch flexible conduit, and #18 TFN wire, which will cut down on your costs; as long as the specs for the job allow this. This is permitted, according to NEC Section 348.20(A)(2); and Sections 402-6, 402-10(2), 240.5(B)(2)).

Now you can take a number of junction boxes (typically 4 inch square boxes) and attach either one, two, three, or four fixture whips to each one. How many of each one you make up will depend on how many of each kind you will need in the job.

Last, you can mount each junction box on the end of a ten foot length of conduit. You can keep separate stacks of these junction boxes, according to how many whips per box. If you know exactly what type of surface they will be attached to, you can even install a fastener in the box at this time too. (A toggle bolt for example).

When you prefab (pre-fabricate) items like this, what you are doing is imitating the assembly line process. You are trying to do as much of the work as possible under the easiest possible conditions. (It is a lot easier to connect fixture whips to a junction box on a workbench than it is on the top of a step ladder; not to mention the time spent gathering all of the materials together).

Almost any time you can prefab your materials you will be better off for it. This is the concept that made Henry Ford wealthy. While the other automobile manufacturers were putting together one car at a time, Ford got enough people together that each one could do only one specific job. This eliminated virtually all of the looking around for materials, and figuring out what the next step was. The old way, the worker had to play both engineer and installer at the same time. Ford had all of the engineering already done, and let the workers be installers only; and further, he kept them supplied with materials so they didn't have to do anything else besides put their piece in the proper place. They made a lot of money.

Of course you can't do this for electrical construction; it is a very different process than building automobiles. But whenever you can use it, you will be better off.

This works especially well for recessed lighting, but don't let that stop you there; if you can find a way to do something like this for another part of your work, do it; it's the little advantages like this that make the difference between profit and loss in electrical construction.

A UNIQUE WAY TO TRIM A PANEL

Making a work of art out of trimming a panel is what we call a "signature item"; a little touch that says you care about the work you do; a little extra to show that your work is first rate.

Doing an immaculate job of trimming out a panel has long been the number one way for an electrician to show what kind of work he does. Here is the most unique way to trim a panel that we know of; it is almost certain to impress those who see it:

First group all of your neutrals and grounding conductors together. Next make two groups of your hot conductors; all the hots that will need to go to the left side of the panel in one group, and all the hots that will go to the right side of the panel in the other group.

Of course you will need to run the heaviest conductors by themselves (typically #8 or larger); do this first, as you normally would. Try to push the heavy wires as far back in the panel as you can, so you have plenty of room for what you are going to do next.

Now, starting with the group of hot wires on the opposite side of the neutral and/or grounding buss, start making a flat braid with the wires. (We'll explain exactly how in just a moment.) Once you have the wires well braided, shape the braid into the panel, so that it follows the gutter space and stays parallel with the panel front.

Now you can take the wires one by one, and bring them into their circuit breakers as they reach them. The wires should come down the side of the panel in the braid, and then peel off one by one as they reach the level of each circuit breaker. The wires should come out of the rear side of the braid, and go straight sideways into the breaker. Of course you will have to narrow the braid towards the bottom, but that isn't really a problem. Please remember to number your wires before you start; trying to trace a wire through a braid isn't real easy.

Now you can do the same thing for the hot wires on the other side of the panel. Follow the same basic pattern. Keep the braid as flat as possible, and parallel with the front of the panel.

Last, do the neutrals and grounds. Depending on the location of the neutral and/or ground buss, you may have to do a little adjusting to make it work right. When you are done, the panel will look very impressive, with colored wire braids running down both sides, and a white braid draped over the top.

Now, here's how to do the braiding:

1. After the wires are grouped together as we said before, work with them to get each wire as straight as possible (we are talking mainly about solid wire now), try to get all of the kinks and bends out. They don't have to be perfect, but if you do a good job of getting them straight, the finished product is better.

2. Clamp the wires together at the top. You will need to do this to get a firm starting point. You can do this pretty easily by using a couple small pieces of wood, and one or two C clamps. Clamp the wires as high as you can in the top of the panel.

3. Now you can start braiding the wires. Remember to keep them flat at all times. We have found that the best way to braid building wires is in groups of 3 or groups of 5. Use groups of 5 as much as you can, as it makes for a wider braid. Do one group at a time, and then you can use a separate wire to braid the groups together when you are done.

A Unique Way To Trim A Panel

To braid the wires you take the outside, wire on one side, and bend it over the top of the other wires, and bring it over 2 wires. Then it will continue downward. Now take the outer-most wire on the other side and bring it over 2 wires, then continue it downward. (For groups of 3 wires you only bring the outside wire over 1 wire.) Go from the top of the group down; the outside wire on one side over two, the outside wire from the other side over two. After you do this a couple of time it gets pretty easy.

4. As you bring the braid down the front of the panel, you will want to start bringing wires into the circuit breakers. Bring your wires out of the braid towards the back. You will want to bring them out at certain places to coordinate with the braiding; so when you bring them out, do it however will make the braid turn out best, and bend them straight up behind the braid (no one can see them this way), bring them up to the proper level, and then bring them across the gutter into the breaker.

5. As you bring the wires out of the braid (you will find, that it usually works well to bring them out two at a time), you will need to change the pattern of the braid. For example: reduce the number of wires in the braid from 5 to 3. Sometimes you will want to combine two braids into one.

For any of these changes. you may need to hide an extra wire (if you have one too many wires for the braid). If so, just keep it tucked behind the braid, and no one will know.

6. After you have your braids arranged where you want them, you can weave a piece of stranded wire (or a smaller size of solid wire) through the braided sets of wires to attach one set to another. By doing this you can make all of the sets of 3 or 5 braided wires into one wide braid. Weave this wire in from the top to the bottom.

7. After you have all the wires into their circuit breakers, straighten out the wires, and flatten them. To really make the job look good, hold a piece of wood behind the braid, and tamp the wires flat with a hammer. Work with the braid for a few minutes until you get it properly situated.

Here are a couple of modifications that will give you a little bit better effect: 1. When you bring a wire out of the braid, add a "dummy" wire of the same color in its place. (By "dummy" wire, we mean that the wire is not used for electricity at all. It is used for cosmetic purposes only.) When you get just past the last wire that comes out of the braid, weave one or two wires sideways across the bottom of the braid to hold it together. Then you can fold it back under itself to give a good finished appearance.

A Unique Way To Trim A Panel

2. You can make your braid all the way to the bottom of the panel, and then a couple of inches. Now you can weave two wires across the braid to hold it together, as we just described. Next, you can bend the whole braid back under itself, and bring each wire up to its proper level, and then bring it across to the circuit breaker. It gives a good effect.

Don't expect to do it perfectly the first time you try; it takes a couple of tries to really get it down. Practice a few times before you try it in a panel; learn how to keep the braid fairly tight and even. Once you learn how to do it well, you can start to experiment with other variations. There is almost no limit to what you can do; try different groupings of colors. etc.

We really like the idea of trimming a panel like this; it really doesn't take too long and it gives the job a lot of class.

FISHING EMT THROUGH BAR JOISTS

This is one way to save a lot of time in installing EMT (thinwall). If you are working in a building where the ceiling is framed with metal bar joists (which is very common), there is a way to fish EMT into the joists; much the same as how you fish cable.

Usually this requires two men working together; here's how to do it:

Have one man work on the ground as a set-up man; he can couple a number of pieces of conduit together while the second man gets his ladder or scaffold set up at the beginning of the run. Then the two men must work together to slide the conduit through the bar joists. Usually this goes pretty smoothly, but sometimes you will have to feed the leading end through the individual joists.

Two men should be able to install a couple of hundred feet of conduit per hour this way. Take care that all of your couplings are good and tight, as they will take more than the usual amount of strain this way.

After you are done sliding the conduit into position, strapping it down is usually a fairly simple proposition. A mineralac type clamp secured by a toggle bolt and washer is fast and easy, as also are the spring steel type beam clamps.

GETTING A THIRD HAND

How many times have you been doing something and needed an extra hand? If you're like most of us, it has probably been quite a few. Here is an idea that can help out a lot:

Take an old spring pole (like the kind they used to use for lighting poles), and when you need a third hand, set up this pole and use it to holding whatever you are working on in place.

Obviously this only works for things you are putting on the ceiling, but it can be very handy. For instance: You can use it when installing lighting tracks on a ceiling, or for installing wiremold.

THE ART OF "SLABBING"

Here are several tips on "slabbing"; that is, installing conduit in concrete floor slabs:

1. Double check the measurements. This is particularly critical when you are trying to hit the middle of an interior wall. (The outside walls are usually pretty easy, as they are well defined; but the inside walls are often not marked before the concrete pour is made; and sometimes they don't end up exactly where the plans say they will be.)

2. Always measure from a permanent reference point: the outside wall, an expansion joint, floor joints, etc.

3. Measure from both ways. If you are measuring to find an interior wall, make your measurements from both ways. Let's say you measure from the outside wall, and mark your location. Then go the other way, and find another reference point; maybe a floor joint or expansion joint; you can even go back to the other wall of the building if you have to. Make a measurement from this point too. You will often find out that the building is a few inches off. Now, you have to find the general contractor, and find out which way he is going to move the wall. Even though you go through an extra step, it's a lot easier and better to do this than to cut up a concrete floor slab.

The Art of Slabbing

4. Make sure that you are on the job site the day the pour is made. Concrete is heavy, and cumbersome to work with, very often the concrete finishers will knock something over in the course of spreading the concrete. Even if they go to the effort of trying to put whatever they knocked around back in place, their chances of getting it exactly correct are not too great. Get a pair of boots like the concrete finishers wear, and wade right in with them. Make sure that all of your equipment is exactly where you want it. An hour later it will be too late.

5. Make sure that all of your conduits are well covered. Concrete is a lot easier to keep out of your pipes than it is to get out when you get around to pulling wire. Remember that your pipes may get knocked down during the pour; and that concrete often gets splashed around quite a bit during the process. Plan for the worst conditions and you won't have trouble later.

(As a note: Duct tape is cheap and works very well. But make sure that you put several layers of tape over the open end of the conduit to give it more strength. If the duct tape were to be punctured or rip, It would be a lot less effective.)

6. Strap your conduits that go up an outside wall. If you can strap these conduits firmly to the wall, and cover them well, you will rarely have any problems with them.

7. In general, make very sure that what you do is correct; double check your work; if there are any locations that are questionable, have the general contractor come over and check them for you. You don't get any second chances in a concrete slab.

To really be good at slabbing takes a little practice. Not only must you figure out where your conduits will have to go, but you must also verify that the building is built correctly (which it usually is not), and compensate for differences between the construction drawings and what you actually find on the job.

Slabbing can save a lot of time and material on the job. (The conduit only has to rise about two feet to a typical receptacle, rather than running up above the ceiling and back down; PVC, which is typically used, is cheaper than EMT; PVC comes with integral couplings, so you don't have to buy or install any couplings; and you can run your conduits a lot more directly. rather than keeping them perpendicular or parallel to ceilings and walls.) But remember that it takes a lot of savings to make up for even one mistake.

Wiring Through A Roof-Top Unit

WIRING THROUGH A ROOF-TOP UNIT

When bringing wiring to a roof-top HVAC unit, the typical method is to run a conduit through the roof (complete with pitch-pan, etc.) and connect it to the unit itself with a piece of liquid tight conduit. Here is a method that is a lot easier and better for all involved:

Typically a large opening with a curb around it is left in the roof for any typical HVAC unit. (HVAC means Heating, Ventilating, and Air Conditioning.) When it arrives, the unit will be set on top of this opening. The unit will have ductwork running to it, which will be run through this opening. This opening will not be full however, there will be unused space. What you can do is to run your conduit to within a foot or two of the unit, and then stop right there until the unit is actually set in place, and the duct work is being run to it. Then you can coordinate with the HVAC installer, and find a place where you can bring your wiring up through the unit itself .

From your conduit, you should run a piece of flexible conduit to the unit (use flexible conduit to avoid any problems with transmitting vibration to the conduit system). In the bottom of the unit, you should cut a hole for your conduit to go through. (Use a knockout cutter to cut a neat hole.) The best way to bring your conduit into the unit is to weld a coupling into the base of the unit. If this isn't feasible for you to do, you can use a close nipple, and secure it to the unit (through the hole that you just cut) with two locknuts. You can then mount a coupling on each side of the nipple, and connect your flex to the couplings with flex connectors.

Once you are inside the unit, it is usually best to continue on with flexible conduit. Depending on what type of unit it is that you are working on, your exact connections once inside the unit will vary.

By running your wiring this way rather than the conventional way, you completely eliminate the pitch-pan, the roof penetration (which makes the roofer's job a lot easier, and makers the roof better, as most roof leaks occur at some type of penetration or edge rather than on the flat parts of the roof), and the need for liquid tight conduit, which is expensive.

You can't do this all the time. Sometimes the roof's characteristics will be such that you can't do this; and sometimes the unit itself will be set up in such a way that it is not feasible. But if you can, it works very well: you do your job better, faster, and cheaper; and the building owner gets a better building.

Patching Holes in Walls

PATCHING HOLES IN WALLS

When putting wiring into existing buildings, you frequentiy have no choice but to make some holes in the walls. Here is some advice on patching these holes:

For large or deep holes use a type of drywall joint compound called "Durabond 90", It sets in 90 minutes, and is very hard and strong. Be careful though that you don't get too much of it in the hole, as it is hard to sand off.

For a final coat, or for a shallow hole you can use regular drywall joint compound, which is easy to work with, and easy to sand.

If you don't have much time, and want the plaster to dry quickly, mix regular drywall joint compound and quick-set plaster together; it will dry very quickly. The more quick-set plaster you use in relation to the joint compound, the faster it will dry.

If you have to patch a hole where you have removed the drywall or plaster completely, this method works well:

Take a scrap piece of drywall a little longer but not quite as wide as the hole (wood would be fine also), and poke a small hole through the center of it with a nail. Next, take a small piece of wood, about the size of a pencil (it doesn't have to be wood, anything will do; actually, a pencil will work great, and is easy to find), and tie a string around it, then push the string through the hole, and pull it up tight.

So now you have a piece of drywall with a string through the middle of it tied to a small piece of wood. Now you want to do this:

Get some construction grade glue, and spread it on the drywall. Put it on the side where the string is sticking out; the opposite side from where the small piece of wood is.

Now, slide this piece of drywall through the hole in the wall, with the glued side facing you. Turn it 90 degrees and pull it back towards you so that it will stick to the back side of the wall. Now tie a longer piece of wood to the string that is hanging out, and twist the longer piece of wood until the piece of drywall is being held firmly in place.

You can walt a couple of hours for the glue to dry, then remove the longer piece of wood and cut off the string. Now you have a firm base to put patching plaster on. Go ahead and patch the hole as you normally would.

USING A CONDUIT BENDER AS A VISE

We've always liked this one. If you look at the illustration, shown on page 40, you will see that the electrician in the drawing is using a regular conduit bender as a vise to hold a piece of conduit while he cuts it.

To do this, you will need a "Benfield" type of bender, which is probably the most common type. (Appleton Electric, Klein Tools, and Ideal Products have been selling them for the past several years, besides the other distribution channels that the Benfield people have used for years.)

Slide the pipe that you want to cut through the rear opening in the bender, then place the bender on a hard surface. Then you can place one

Using A
Conduit
Bender
As A Vise

knee on the handle of the bender as shown in the drawing to hold it firmly. Then you can go ahead and cut your pipe.

We really like this little trick, as it can save a lot of running around looking for something to cut a pipe on. It really works well – try it.

Using a conduit bender as a vise

COMBINING A TIME CLOCK AND A PHOTO-CELL FOR LIGHTING CONTROL

Here is a good way to get customized lighting control without going to an expensive controller:

By wiring a photo-cell (photo-electric control) in series with a standard time clock, you can set up your controls so that the lights will turn on whenever it gets dark outside, except when you don't want them to be on.

As you see in the accompanying drawings, power first comes in to the time clock (which must always have power to keep the time), and then the hot lead of the photo-cell is fed from the load side of the time clock. The neutrals of course feed through from one neutral terminal to another; and the lighting is fed from the load side of the photo-cell with the neutral fed through to the light fixtures also.

This differs from the typical use of time clocks in that time clocks are usually thought of as for turning something on at a specified time. In this set-up however, we are using the time clock to turn the circuit off and using the photo-cell to turn it on.

A typical set-up would be something like this:

After both the time clock and photo-cell are properly mounted, the time clock will be set to turn on at 9:00 a.m., and set to turn off at 8:00 p.m. So at 9:00 a.m. power is fed from the time clock to the photo-cell, and at 8:00 p.m. this power is cut off. So then, at any time between 9:00 a.m. and 8:00 p.m. if the photo-cell senses darkness, the lights will turn on (thus, the lights will turn on not only in the dark of the evening, but also if the sky is darkened because of a storm, etc.); and between 8:00 p.m. and 9:00 a.m. there will be no power fed to the lights under any circumstances (to conserve energy).

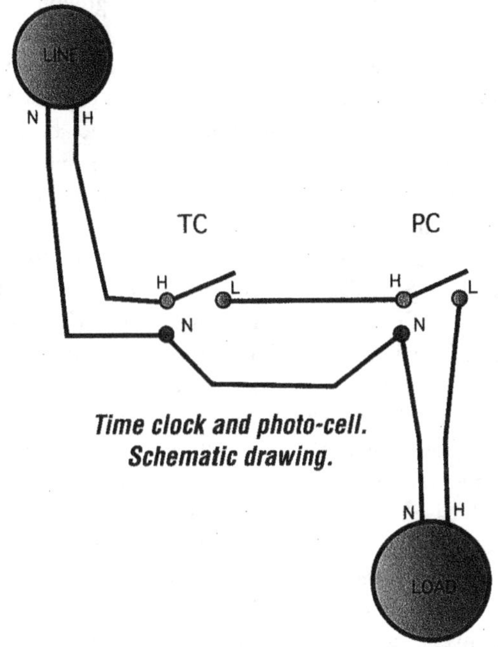

Time clock and photo-cell. Schematic drawing.

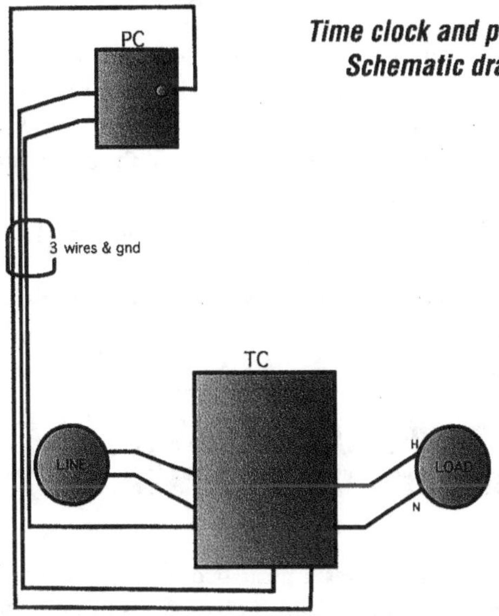

Time clock and photo-cell. Wiring diagram.

Combining A Time Clock & A Photo-cell

GETTING A VERY LOW RESISTANCE GROUND UNDER POOR SOIL CONDITIONS

With the widespread use of sensitive electronic and computerized equipment, the need of a good, low resistance grounding electrodes has become far more important than it used to be. In many areas however, it is very dIfficuit to get a low resistance ground because of the soil conditions (i.e., sandy soils).

One answer is to drive more ground rods, and bury a counterpoise; but this doesn't always work well, and is expensive.

Here is the best way we know of to get a really good ground:

Around your ground rod (or ground rod!) dig a trench about two feet deep, and one foot wide. This trench should be about two feet outside of the ground rod(s).

Then, in the bottom of the trench you should spread a few inches of Rock Salt. The standard type of Rock Salt that is used for water softeners is fine; but you can also use calcium chloride, or magnesium chloride (which is supposed to be the best). Last, fill the trench back up.

Getting A Good Ground In Poor Soil

What this does is ionize the moisture in the soil, which makes it conduct electricity far better.

You should add more salt about once every year; and one more thing to remember is this: because of salt's corrosive characteristics, you will have to replace your ground rod(s) every five to ten years; and with the ground rod(s) should also be replaced that portion of the grounding conductor which lies within five to ten feet of the salt.

This method should, be able to get you a ground with about two ohms of resistance or less in almost any type of soil.

Give the area a good watering right after you do this the first time to get the ionization started.

HOW THE "FLATTERS" COULD HANG 700 FEET OF PIPE PER DAY WITH NO POWER TOOLS

Just after World War II there was a great boom in construction, especially residential construction. At this time there were still a number of areas in the country where the use of cable was not an acceptable wiring method (even today there remain a few areas where cable is not allowed); because of this, in these areas every new residence had EMT with individual conductors for its wiring.

Because of these conditions, there were certain electricians that specialized in this type of work; these electricians (at least the ones we've known) referred to themselves as "flatters". (The terms "flatters" and "flatting" come from the old word for apartment or floor--flat.)

Because these electricians specialized in this type of work, they developed some very specific techniques for installing their conduit (EMT) which enabled them to install a tremendous amount of pipe per day. The figure we've mentioned so far is 700 feet per day; this however was only a mediocre amount for these men, as we knew one fellow who used to hang 1000 feet of pipe on a good day.

Here is a description of their technique, as it was described to us:

"First thing. we did was nail up all the boxes--all at the same height--receptacles all the same height; switches all the same height, light fixtures in the center of the room. Everything was fed from the top down--like an octopus."

"Then we bend all of the drops to the switches and outlets; all the same. You know--you measure the distance from the top of the box to the top of the joists, add about two inches, and bend them so they are that long; all the drops to the switches the same, and all the drops to the receptacles the same. You cut open all your bundles of pipe and push the ends up against the wall, so all of them are even; then you draw a line across all of them at the right place, and that's where you bend them. You can do it pretty fast after you get used to it."

"Then you take a chisel and make notches where you have to go through the top plate. I had a big chisel, about 2-1/2 inches wide-kept it real sharp. You gave the chisel two good hits, one on one side of the notch, one on the other; then you take your hammer and knock out the wood. It was a lot faster than these special saws that I see these guys using now (reciprocating saws, or "Sawzalls" --ed.); three hits and we were done. We didn't need a ladder or anything, you just reach up and give it a good whack."

"Then you go ahead and put in all the drops; you spin a connector on the box, slide your pipe in the connector, screw it tight, and nail up a strap at the top plate. I always had everything I needed on me; I had an apron like the carpenters use; I kept all my connectors, couplings, nails, and straps in it. My tape measure too--everything."

The Old-Time Flatters

"After you get all of the drops in, you start tying everything into the ceiling boxes; all the branch circuits go through the ceiling boxes. Then you run your home runs: we always ran one to the bedrooms, one for the kitchen, and one to the rest of the house. (Note that a modern house would need many more circuits than this, as modern homes need a lot more power than those which were constructed 30 or 40 years ago. --ed.) Last, we ran the range circuit, and the circuits to the dryer and heater if they weren't gas."

One interesting thing to observe about the flatters is that their bosses did a very good job of supplying them. Of course this was a lot easier to do back then, as there were fewer parts that went into a wiring job; and also that these men specialized in one specific type of job. Regardless of this though, the contractors had everything on the job waiting for the men; they didn't waste a lot of time looking around for materials.

None of these techniques are very difficult or revolutionary, but these men took advantage of what they knew, and used them very well. A lot of modern electricians, and especially electrical contractors, could learn a good lesson from the flatters.

Cable Dish

USING A "CABLE DISH"

This idea is for the guys who do a lot of residential wiring; specifically with Romex (Type NM Cable).

This cable comes in either cartons of 250 feet or in 1000 foot reels. The cartons are difficult to use because the cable gets twisted when it comes out of the box, and the reels are tough because they are so heavy and difficult to maneuver.

Here is an idea some electricians in South Florida came up with a number of years back:

Take a piece of plywood and from it cut as many circles as you can with a diameter of 18-20 inches. (Use 5/8" outdoor grade plywood).

Then into the center of each one put in an eye screw. To the" eye screw attach a swivel snap (like the end of a dog's leash), and to that about 3 feet of chain. Last, on the end of the chain, attach a big hook. Bending a piece of aluminum stock to size is probably the cheapest and easiest way.

When you go in to a new house that you are wiring, take one of these cable dishes for each type of cable you will use, and place the cable

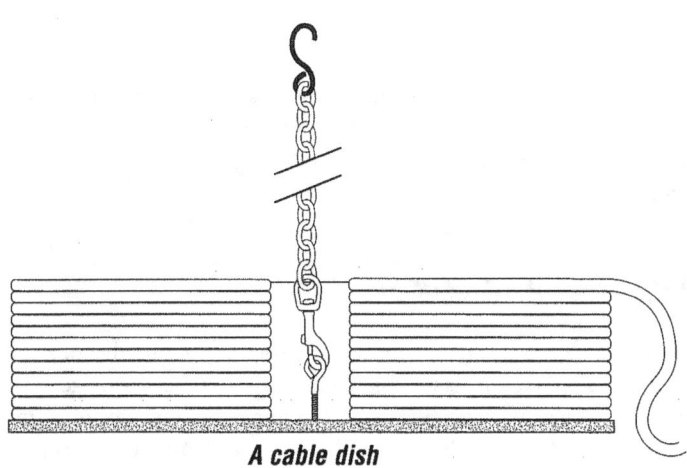

A cable dish

on the dish, and then just hang it up on one of the joists. When you pull the end of the cable the dish turns, and the cable comes off smooth and easy; no kinks, and no tugging. See above diagram.

It helps if you put a little oil or grease on the swivel snap; also, you should slip a piece of PVC conduit over the chain and snap to prevent the cable from getting torn up when it brushes up against the center of the dish.

Using Stilts To Install Cable

USING STILTS TO INSTALL CABLE

This idea is perfect for residential installations where type NMB or type AC cable is used; but you could probably apply it to a hundred other situations with equally good results.

Get a pair of stilts like the drywall installers use. You can buy them at most good contractor supply houses for about $250.00; if you have trouble finding them, call a drywall or plastering contractor and find out where they get theirs.

Stilts take a little while to get used to, so practice a few times with someone standing by watching you before you go out on your own.

Set up the stilts so that when you stand on them, the top of your head is just below the bottom of the joists. You'll find that once you get used to is, you can almost run through the house stringing cable.

Be sure to have all of your boxes mounted, and notches cut before you get up on the stilts, then you can work unhindered. Also remember to keep the straps on your stilts as tight as you can; it makes a difference. Remember, too, to be careful, especially your first five or ten times on the stilts--a fall from two feet off the ground hurts a lot more than a normal fall.

SECTIONAL BAG FOR FITTINGS

We met an electrician in Chicago who used to do a number of small to medium sized jobs. As is typical of almost all electricians who go from job to job, he had a real problem with running out of one type of fitting or another, and wasting hours running back and forth to the supply house for one or two items.

Fortunately, Frank's wife was somewhat of a seamstress, and came up with an idea that has served Frank well for many years. She made him a special canvas bag for all of the small items that Frank had such trouble keeping up on (connectors, couplings, straps, grounding pig-tails, etc.).

As you look at the sketch of the bag (shown below), you see that there are a number or sections; how many sections, and how deep each one is will be your own decision based upon what types of material you commonly use.

Here is one thing to remember: Use enough canvas so that when you set the bag down, it will open up wide, and almost lay flat. This way, you can go on the job and just lay the bag down; then all your fittings will be in one easy-to-find place.

Also, put a rope through the top hem of the bag so that when you get ready to go, all you have to do is to pick up the rope and the whole bag folds together neatly; you can just pick it up and go.

Remember to make the bag out of good, strong canvas, strong thread, and high quality rope. You will want this bag to last for many years, so make it right.

RUTH'S WORK APRON

This is probably the best work apron we've ever seen for electricians. An electrician who did a lot of office renovation work got his wife (named Ruth, obviously) to make this for him. He says that it is absolutely the best work apron he's ever seen, and that it has saved him a lot of time and hassles.

As you look at the drawing shown at right, you see that the apron has a number of oversized pockets; they are about 5 inches wide and 6 inches deep. Note also that these pockets are a little bit larger at the bottom than they are at the top. This is so when you lean over to pick something. up, all your fittings, etc. won't fall out of the pockets.

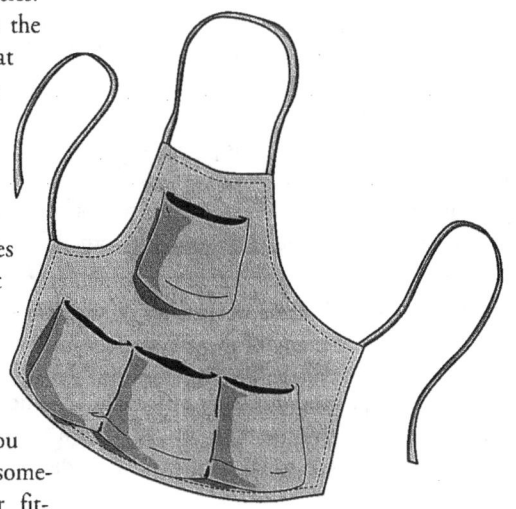

The best work apron

Ruth's husband says that he can get almost a full box of connectors or couplings in one of these pockets. He likes using one pocket for connectors, one for couplings, one for straps, and one for a tape measure and pencils when he is roughing-in; and when he does his trimout, he loads up the apron with wire nuts, pigtails, switches, receptacles, and plates.

The apron should be made out of a good grade of canvas; and be sure to use a fairly wide piece for the strap around the neck to make it as comfortable as possible.

HOW TO GREASE MOTOR BEARINGS WHILE THE MOTOR IS RUNNING

Almost any factory electrician is familiar with the conflicts between production and maintenance. Often, a piece of equipment that needs service cannot be shut down to get this service because doing so would shut down an entire production line, and cost the company a vast amount of money; so the maintenance must wait until a more convenient time, which doesn't always come very quickly.

Here is a good way to grease your motors with greaseable bearings without having to shut them down:

First, remove both the top and bottom plugs. Then add grease into the top fitting. Add new grease until the grease that comes out of the bottom fitting is clean. Then replace the bottom plug, but leave the top plug off still. Let the motor operate as normal for 10 or 15 minutes; by that time any extra grease will have worked itself out of the top opening. Now you can go ahead and close up the top plug also.

Take care that any of the grease that you force out of the bearing, or that leaks out of the bearing does not get into the windings of the motor, as the grease can damage the motor's windings. Also be careful that no dirt gets into the bearing while you have the top plug removed so the excess grease can work its way out of the bearing.

RUNNING A THREE PHASE MOTOR WITH A SINGLE PHASE POWER

A three phase motor can be run on single phase power by the use of capacitors to create a type of rotating magnetic field in all three windings of the motor.

If you refer to the drawing on page 49, you will see that one leg of the single phase power is connected to one motor lead, and the other single phase leg is connected to another of the three phase motor's leads. The third motor lead is run first to a capacitor. and then back to one of the single phase leads.

As you notice. there are two capacitors shown in this drawing; one is a "run" capacitor, meaning that it is in the circuit at all times. The other is a "start" capacitor, which is used only for a few seconds at start-up; this is necessary to provide the extra torque that is needed to start the motor. The run capacitor should be an oil type capacitor as it will be carrying a significant amount of current, and needs to be hefty enough to take a fair amount of heat. This run capacitor should be sized at 25 to 30 mfd per horsepower. The starting capacitor can be of the electrolytic type (which is cheaper), as it will only be in the circuit for a few seconds. This start capacitor should be sized at about 60 mfd per horsepower.

If you have any trouble finding capacitors of the right size, remember that you can "stack" your capacitors; that is, you can hook them up in parallel. Capacitors connected in parallel are additive (a 30 mfd capacitor and a 40 mfd capacitor hooked up in parallel equal 70 mfd); so this should eliminate any such problems.

Three phase motor set up to operate on single phase power

To operate your motor manually you will need a regular start switch (single pole, normally open, momentary contact), and wire it into the circuit as shown above. You must push your start switch, then turn on your single phase power, and then let off of your start switch after the motor is up to speed. On page 50 we are showing a three phase motor being run on single phase power in this same way, but with an automatic (magnetic) starter.

Because one leg of this three phase power is being made by the use of capacitors, you can get some very unbalanced currents. Because of this, a motor run on this set-up should not be run at more than 75% of its full load for an extended period of time.

Below we are showing a variation of this method which also incorporates an autotransformer to balance the currents better.

You will need to experiment with the autotransformer to find out which of its taps would be the best to use, but using the autotransformer will give you a much more efficient operation. Using this set-up you can run motors up to 100 horsepower or more, if necessary.

If properly adjusted, this set-up will operate extremely well at full load, with current in all three legs equally balanced. At no load however, its operation is not too good.

Running A Three Phaste Motor On Single Phase Power

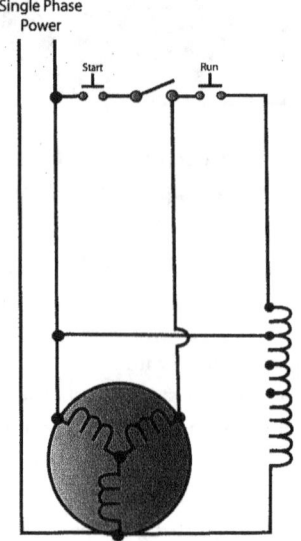

Three phase motor operating on single phase power using an autotransformer.

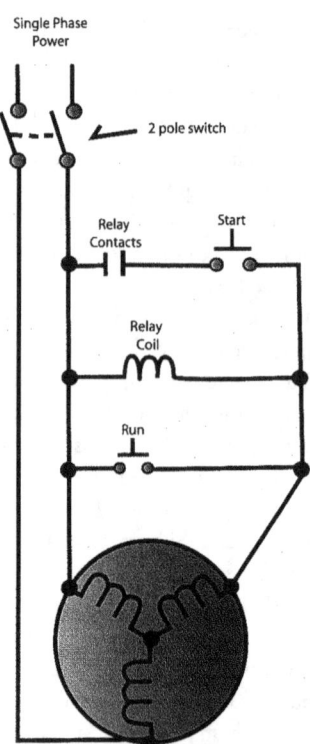

Three phase motor operating on single phase power using a magnetic starter.

One note about autotransformers: Autotransformers can be kind of tricky, so handle them with care. Make sure that the autotransformer that you use is rated for the amounts of current and voltage that it will be required to carry.

Also remember that the voltage rating of your three phase motor must match the voltage of your single phase supply.

USE OF A BARE GROUNDING CONDUCTOR TO PROTECT AGAINST GROUND FAULTS

Here is something we learned from one of the top engineering companies in Florida: When PVC conduit is used for underground runs (and it is now used the majority of the time for such installations), you run the risk of having ground faults that will not be detected.

This is why: Almost any underground PVC electrical conduit will have water seep into it in the course of time (usually in a very short time). Because of this, the conductors will have a direct connection to ground. This contact to ground is not a problem in itself, but the problem is this: if the insulation in one of the hot conductors breaks down, cracks, or gets scraped off during its installation, there will be no return path to the panel in which the circuit originates. This means that the fault current will run through the ground rather than returning through the conduit.

When the fault current returns through the conduit, there is usually very little resistance in the path of the current, and the fuse or circuit breaker will do its job and cut off power to that circuit. But if the fault current must go through the earth itself, there is a lot of resistance for it to go through before it can get back to the panel. So the earth itself will carry the current; and further, there is no way to tell where this stray current (and voltage) will go; it could cause some dangerous situations.

Using A Bare Grounding Conductor

Of course there is a grounding conductor run with any underground circuit that is in PVC conduit; but this doesn't really help very much, because this conductor is almost always insulated. So the grounding conductor will not carry any of the current from an underground fault unless it has a void in its own insulation; also, this void would have to be very close to the insulation void in the hot conductor to do much good.

So, our associate from the engineering company says that they always specify a bare copper grounding conductor for any runs of PVC conduit that are below grade. This way, if there is a fault, the bare grounding conductor will pick up the fault current as well or better than a metallic conduit would.

We think the engineering company has a very good point.

A FAST METHOD FOR INSTALLING EMT ABOVE SUSPENDED CEILINGS

This method can be used for most sizes of EMT above most types of suspended ceilings. It works very well with the "inverted T" ceiling; which is the most common type. This technique is especially good for long, straight runs; but can also be a great help for installing runs with bends also.

Here is the basic technique: Set up your scaffold or ladder at one end of the run. Make sure you have plenty of pipe and plenty of couplings with you. After you remove one or two panels of the ceiling, lay your first piece of pipe on top of the suspended ceiling. Now attach a coupling to the end of the pipe (set-screw types work best). Next, pull up another piece of pipe, and attach it to this coupling, and push the pieces of conduit in the direction of the run until the new piece of conduit is laying where the first one was a moment ago. The first piece will now be 10 feet further towards the end of the run.

You can continue this process until you get to about 250 feet (for 1/2 inch EMT), after which the process becomes more difficult. As you push each successive piece, you will find it necessary to twist the conduit as you push it on toward the end of the run; as long as you make up your couplings good and tight, you should have no problem with this.

After you get your conduit as far as you want it to go, you can start strapping it up (approx. every 10 feet). The easiest way to do this is to use a special type of strap that is specifically designed for the suspended ceiling system. The CADDY® company makes severel such products (as do a few other manufacturers). While formally one could use a product called the CADDY® "KON-SLIP" which was a perfect adjunct to running wire over suspended ceilings by utilizing the suspension ties of the ceiling, this method is no longer permitted in the NEC. Now, electricians must support their wires by hanging independent suspension ties which are not part of the ceiling system. If you use this type of fastener, you can follow the run, just stopping momentarily at the location of each strap.

Installing EMT this way is very fast; we've seen a run of over 200 feet installed in about 1-1/2 hours; by one man. This method would also work well with any other type of conduit. However, Rigid steel conduit would be pretty hard to work with, and we don't really like the idea of using PVC in a ceiling space; so we think that using EMT for this type of installation is best, and certainly the most common.

USING A 2 X 2 FLOOR GRID AS A HIGH FREQUENCY GROUND

The real problem with getting a good computer ground is that computers operate at a very high frequency; typically measured in mega-hertz (one mega-hertz equals one million cycles per second). As the frequency of an AC current goes up, so does its inductive reactance, which is proportional to the frequency.

The formula for inductive reactance is this:

$$X_L = 2 \pi f L$$

So the inductive reactance (called XL and measured in ohms) is equal to 2 times 11 (which is 2 times 3.1416, or 6.2832), times frequency (0, times the inductance of the conductor which carries the current (L).

So if we have a computer that operates at a speed of 4 mega-hertz (MHz), and a number 8 AWG grounding conductor which is 50 feet long between the computer and the grounding electrode (ground rod or other), the resistance of the grounding conductor will be 414 ohms! That means that if the grounding conductor picks up a current of 10 volts (which is high for a computer), approximately 24 milliamps of current will be allowed to flow through the #8 grounding conductor. At 5 volts, which is more common, just about 12 milliamps will flow through the grounding system.

Here is how we come up with these numbers:

First of all, we know that 11 equals 3.1416. Next, we know that the frequency is 4 MHz, or 4,000,000 cycles per second. Now, we calculate the inductance of the wire: #8 wire has an inductive reactance (reactance is almost the same thing as resistance; in fact, you can think of reactance as AC resistance. Reactance plus resistance equals impedance, measured in ohms) of .656 ohms per mile at 60 cycles. At 4,000,000 cycles, this figure would be 43,733 ohms per mile. Since 50 feet is .00947 of a mile; the inductive reactance of this piece of wire is 414.15 ohms. (.00947 x 43,733 = 414.15).

So we see that at this frequency, our grounding system is not very effective. The main factor here is the length of the conductor, not the size of the conductor. As long as the wire is large enough that it won't melt under a fault current (which makes almost any size of building wire adequate for a computer, which uses relatively little current) the size matters very little.

Using A 2x2 Floor For A High Frequency Ground

(As a note: It sometimes helps -to use a flat, or flat braided conductor because they have a larger surface area than a round conductor. High frequency currents flow more on the outside skin of the conductor than they do in the middle of the conductor. This is commonly called skin effect. We note this for your information, but it really isn't a critical factor for the grounding of a small computer.)

One answer to this problem is to bring a high quality ground up to the computer itself. This can be done by using a transformer to create a separate system of supply in the vicinity. Some of the better "Computer Power Centers" do this. The problem with this is the distance factor if you have more than one computer. What happens if you have a computer room with ten computers? If you set up a separate source of supply for each computer, you will run up a big bill very quickly.

About the best answer that we have heard is to use the 2 x 2 flooring system that most large computer rooms use as a grounding grid.

The reason we like this idea is this: The more paths for a current to take, the less resistance. If you give a certain voltage only one path at a certain voltage, a certain amount of current will flow (which can be figured using ohm's law). If you give the same voltage four current paths (all identical to the first), four times as much current will flow; or you can say it in reverse: the resistance drops to one fourth of what it was.

When you use the flooring system as a grounding grid, and ground the grid at several locations; you create a high number of paths for the ground current to travel. Being as the 2 x 2 flooring grid is made out of substantial sized pieces of steel, the resistance of the grid will be fairly low; actually, it may be effectively less than copper wire due to its much larger surface area.

The only modification needed for the flooring grid is to make sure the joints of the grid will conduct the current well. The only good way to check this is with an ohm meter. Each joint should have less than one ohm of resistance from one side to the other. Any joints with more. than this amount of resistance should be corrected; this usually entails a jumper, soldering, or some other form of electrical connection.

Make sure that the flooring grid is grounded at several locations; the more the better. Each computer should be grounded directly to the flooring grid. Use the shortest possible piece of wire between the computer and the grid.

You can refer to Article 645 of the National Electric Code for further requirements.

USING TEMPLATES

Using templates to arrange the location of conduits can be a big help in electrical construction projects; not so much for saving time, but rather for avoiding lost time.

The typical scenario goes like this: An electrical contracting company gets a certain project. They go through the processes of ordering all of their materials, preparing submittals, etc. After a little while they get their submittals approved, and place the order for their materials to be delivered. In the meanwhile the general contractor is getting ready to pour the concrete for the floor slab. He calls the electrical contractor, and notifies him that he has one week to have all of his slab work complete.

Now the electrical contractor is in a hurry to get all of his under slab work done; but he has a problem: There are 17 conduits, ranging from 1 inch to 4 inch that feed into the bottom of the main distribution panel. Of course, there is no way to get the distribution panel on the job site before the slab is poured; so the only answer is to get some engineering drawings from the switchgear manufacturer, and make a template of the knockout locations on the bottom of the distribution panel.

Using Templates

Most of the manufacturers can get these drawings for you pretty easily. Make sure though, that they double check and verify that the drawings they show you are indeed the way the equipment will actually be built; mistakes like this have happened before.

You will probably find it best to make your template out of 1/2 to 5/8 inch plywood (outdoor grade). Also be sure that you've got the distances from the walls correct, including any finish that the walls will get; a 1/2 inch mistake makes a big difference.

As always, make sure that you plug the open ends of your conduits to prevent any concrete or anything else from getting into them; and make sure that you have a man on the site the day the slab is poured, so in case the concrete finishers mess up your pipes, you will have a man there to fix them before the concrete dries and there is nothing you can do. Leave the template on the conduits while the pour is made for best results.

CHEAP AND AVAILABLE EXPANSION JOINTS

Expansion joints can be expensive; and what is worse than that, is that they can be very hard to find.

If you run into a situation where you need an expansion joint but just can't get one when you want it, here's one method that will work equally well:

At the location where the expansion joint is supposed to go, mount two junction boxes about a foot apart. In between these two junction boxes, run a piece of flexible conduit (Greenfield), sized the same as the conduit that it is connecting. For outdoor work use "Seal-tite" conduit (Liquidtight) with proper fittings. When you install your wires, leave loops in them to allow for any expansion or contraction. This method is actually better than the manufactured expansion joint as far as allowing movement.

Expansion Joints

One thing to remember when you do this: Make sure you run a properly sized equipment grounding conductor in the flexible conduit, and connect it to the raceway system on each end. You can find out how to size these conductors by referring to Section 250.122, and Table 250.122 of the National Electrical Code.

RUNNING POWER TOOLS FROM YOUR AUTOMOBILE ALTERNATOR

This is a slick little trick that can really save you a lot of time; especially for new projects in out of the way places where there is no power available.

Remember however, that this power that you will be using is not regular AC power, it is DC. The reason you can use it to run your power tools is that almost all power tools use a universal type motor, which can be used equally well on either AC or DC. Do not try to run anything on this power that needs alternating current. For instance, if someone else on the job plugs their radio into this power supply, they will probably burn up their radio in short order. The DC current will rush through the power supply transformer at a high amperage without the inductive reactance that would be present in the circuit if the current were 60 Hz AC. In most cases this small transformer would only last for a number of seconds, probably a minute at the most. So, be careful; not only for yourself, but for others also.

An automobile alternator is very simple in operation: the rotor is wound with a coil of wire, and rotates according to the speed of the engine. The rotor coil gets power from the battery through two slip rings. As the rotor travels through the alternator, it induces a voltage into the stator's windings, which are wound the same as is a three phase motor. Actually, the power that the automobile alternator initially puts out is three phase. However, after it is generated, it is converted to DC by means of a full wave three phase rectifier.

The voltage that an alternator like this would put out is dependent upon the speed of the rotor; the faster the rotor's movement, the higher the voltage; the lower the rotor's movement, the lower the voltage. This isn't very good for the automobile's operation though, so a voltage regulator is used to keep the alternator's output at just about 12 volts. What this voltage regulator does is to cut down on the amount of current flowing through the rotor's windings. This is done by adding a resistance in series with the rotor. A voltage divider circuit is used to check the output voltage and regulate the amount of current that will be allowed to flow through the rotor. Believe it or not, the circuitry isn't really that hard, but we won't go through it in this book.

In order to get the alternator to put out 120 volts, you have to bypass the voltage regulator; so that the rotor will get the full 12 volts that the battery puts out at all times. Now the rotor will get the full current at all times and all you have to do is to increase the engine's speed until the alternator's output reaches 120 volts. Also, you will have to transfer the alternator's output current from the automobile circuit to a receptacle that you can plug in to.

The best way to do this is to first bypass the voltage regulator by putting a single pole switch from the positive side of the battery (you can pick up a wire that is connected to the positive side of the battery at the voltage regulator if you want to) to the rotor field in the alternator (often identified as terminal F). When this switch is open, the voltage regulator will operate normally; but when you close it, power will go directly from the battery to the rotor field at 12 volts. Although the regulator will continue to operate, a completely independent and unrestricted path for

Running Power Tools From Your Automobile Alternator

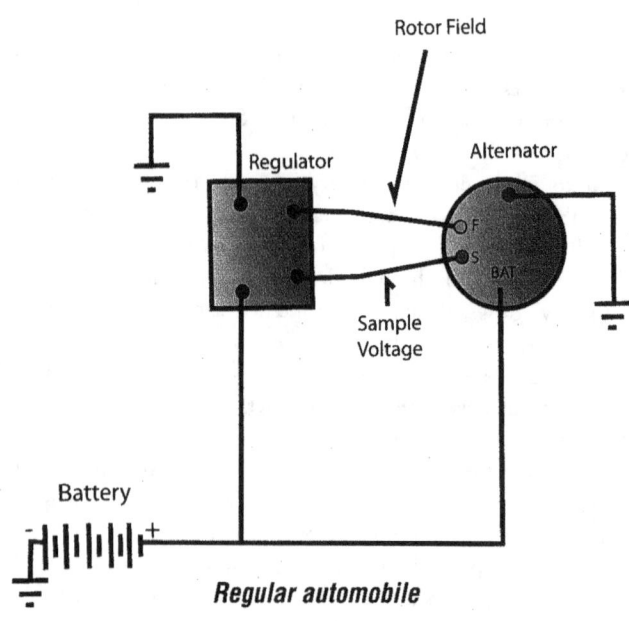

Regular automobile

the rotor current is established. Now, the faster you run the engine, the higher voltage your alternator will put out.

The other thing you will need to do is to install another single pole switch between the alternator terminal marked "S" and the wire that leads from this terminal to the voltage regulator. This terminal and wire feed the sample output voltage of the alternator to the voltage regulator. It is a good idea to put this switch in the circuit so that you can disconnect the sample circuit from the regulator when it will be operated at a high voltage; there may be some parts in your alternator that won't handle the high voltage.

The next thing you need to do is to transfer the alternator's output from the automobile circuit to the receptacle(s) that you want to use. This is best done with a single pole, double throw switch; which is the same thing as a three-way switch, but a little better built. You can use a spec grade three-way switch if you need to. The common terminal of this switch should be connected to the alternator terminal typically marked "BAT", meaning that this is the alternator's output terminal, which is connected to the positive side of the battery. Of the other terminals of this switch; one side should be connected to the regulator to feed it 12 volt

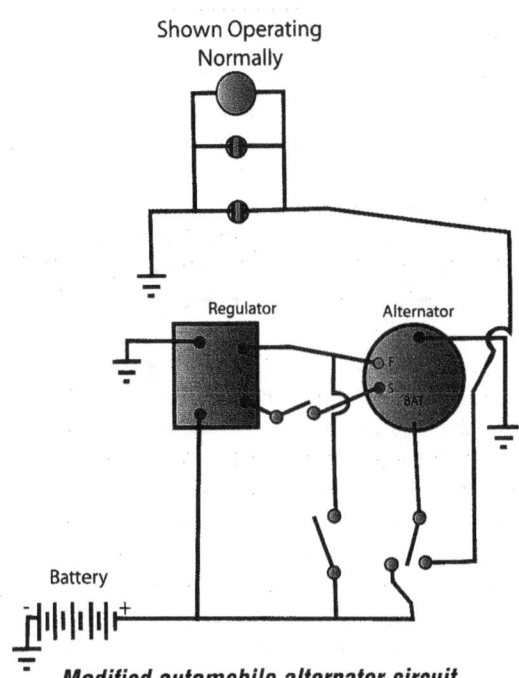

Modified automobile alternator circuit

power directly from the battery as it got before we put this switch in its way. The other terminal should be connected first to a fuse (20 to 30 amp would be a good range), and then to a DC volt meter and your receptacle, or group of receptacles. A drawing of this is shown above.

These outlets, and the voltmeter should also be connected to ground as shown. As for all auto wiring, the vehicle's frame serves as a ground terminal.

Here are several important things to remember when you set up a system like this:

Not all alternators and voltage regulators are the same. What we are explaining here are typical situations; check a good manual (like Chilton's), and make sure your alternator and voltage regulator are set up this way before you try. (Most are, but it is worth your time to check).

Use high quality switches. These switches will be required to carry quite a bit of DC current, which is a lot harder on switches than AC current is. Use DC rated switches if at all feasible. If you have to, you can probably get away with spec grade AC switches.

Running Power Tools From Your Automobile Alternator

DO NOT throw any of these switches unless the engine is turned off. If you do, you are running the risk of burning up your automobile wiring by giving it an unregulated voltage. Park the vehicle where you will want it; turn it off; throw your switches; then start it up again.

If you use regular three prong, grounding receptacles, make sure that you install a jumper from the neutral terminal to the ground terminal of the receptacle. This is to insure that any ground-fault current will have a low resistance path to take; rather than traveling through the person holding the tool.

You will have to rev the engine up some to get 120 volts. This is the reason we are showing a volt meter in the circuit. Rev the engine up until you get 120 volts. You can then adjust the choke to keep the engine idling at this speed. Don't let the engine fall below this speed, as too low of a voltage can burn up a motor quickly.

Use only a high temperature wire for these connections; they should be oil resistant as well. As always, make good connections.

Don't run this system for more than a couple of hours. By setting up the system" this way, your battery puts out power, but doesn't get any back. Theoretically. the battery should be able to take this type of operation for over 10 hours; but we don't advise that you get anywhere close to that figure. An automobile battery can be severely damaged if completely discharged.

If you've got enough space under the hood of your car or truck, you could mount everything right under the hood. If you do, make sure that you use wiring materials that are oil resistant and water resistant; as they may be subjected to a lot more environmental difficulties than they would inside a building.

Using A Ladder As A Work Station

USING A LADDER AS A WORK STATION

If you want to save time when roughing-in conduit, this is one of the best ways to do it. Although many of us now use fiberglass ladders and obviously OSHA may have a problem with altering the stingers on a ladder, I decided to include this "secret" as a nod to our "old-school" brethren.

First, cut a couple of notches in the side rails of a step ladder just above the second step. By doing this, you can place a conduit in these notches, kneel on the pipe, and cut it easily. These notches should be cut in a trian-

Using a ladder as a work station

gular shape with one side flush with the second step of the ladder. When you slide a conduit into these notches, it should rest on the second step.

The next thing to do, is to hang two hooks on the side of the ladder, near the top. If you are right handed, put these hooks on the right side of the ladder; and if you are left handed, put them on the left. side of the ladder. Put one hook on the front side rail of the ladder (the side that typically has steps rather than rungs), and one hook (a pretty large one) on the rear side rail, lower on the ladder. You will use the front hook for your hacksaw, and the larger rear hook for your pipe bender.

Cutting a conduit using notches in ladder as a vise

By doing this, you arrange all of the items that you need to work with to be almost at your finger tips. Additionally, if you use good sized hooks, you can pick up the ladder with the hack saw and bender still hanging on it, and take it to your next location. See the illustrations on pages 61.

One other thing that you can do along these lines is to hang a canvas bag on the other side of the ladder. In the bag you can put whatever types of materials that you are working with at the time: boxes, fittings, plaster rings t straps, other tools, etc. If you use a canvas bag like this, you would do well to make sure the bag is mounted loosely enough that it can swing a little bit, so when you pick up the ladder to move it the contents of the bag don't fall out.

It also works very well to do something like this with a scaffold. You can build racks on the sides of the platform that you can use for pipe, boxes, fittings, wire, even light fixtures. There are any number of possible set-ups; you can design your own for your individual needs.

Analyzing The Leads Of A Nine Lead Motor

HOW TO ANALYZE THE LEADS OF A NINE LEAD MOTOR

This is a way to identify the leads on a standard nine lead motor, even if the numbers are not marked on the wires. We learned it from an old Navy electrician.

First, you should know how these leads are numbered. On page 63 you will see diagrams of exactly how these wires are numbered. Wires number 1, 2, and 3 are the wires that you will always connect line voltage to. Notice in the upper drawing that the wires for a wye wound motor are numbered in a clockwise spiral. For a delta wound motor, the numbers also go clockwise: corners first, then the left sides of: the coils, then the right sides of the coils last.

Nine lead motors are designed to work on either of two voltages; typically 240 volts and 480 volts. Nine lead motors are also called dual-voltage motors. You notice in these drawings that this type of motor actually has two coils of wire per phase; if these coils of wire are connected in series, They will be set up for the higher of their two voltages; if they are connected in parallel, they will be set up for the lower of their two voltages. You can see this in the diagram on page 63.

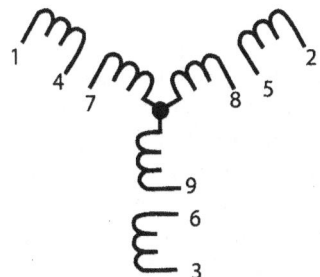

Numbering of leads for a wye wound motor

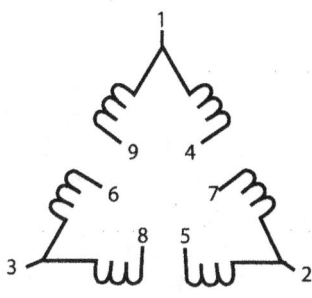

Numbering of leads for a delta wound motor

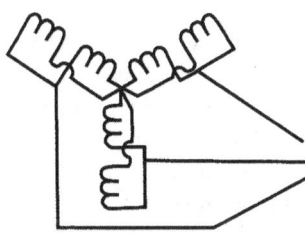

Wye wound motor set up for 240 volt operation

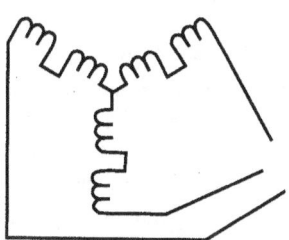

Wye wound motor set up for 480 volt operation

Delta wound motor set up for 240 volt operation

Delta wound motor set up for 480 volt operation

Analyzing The Leads Of A Nine Lead Motor

Let's assume this motor is typical; that is, it is set up to operate on 240 or 480 volts. In the center left diagram on page 63 the motor is connected for 240 volts. You notice that line voltage is connected not only to wires number 1, 2, and 3; but there are jumpers from 1 to 7, 2 to 8, and 3 to 9. You also see that wires number 4, 5, and 6 are connected together to make a second star point. This way each coil gets a separate source of 240 volt power. What you have is actually two separate motor circuits operating from the same voltage source.

Now if you look at the lower drawings, you see the same motor set up for 480 volts. This time the coils are connected in parallel, and 480 volts is connected to terminals number 1, 2, and 3; with jumpers between terminals number 4 and 7; 5 and 8; and 6 and 9. The way this motor is set up now, each pair of coils gets 480 volts. Since these coils are identical, each coil will get 240 volts, the same as in the low voltage connection.

On page 63 we are showing the same connections for a delta connected motor. In the upper drawing you see that the 240 volt line connects to terminals 1, 2, and 3; with jumpers between terminals number 1, 6, and 7; 2, 4, and 8; and 3, 5, and 9. If you trace this circuitry, you will find out that just as in the wye connected motor, each coil receives a separate supply of 240 volts. In the lower right drawing, you see the delta motor set up for 480 volts. As always, the line voltage connects to terminals number 1, 2, and 3; and we place jumpers between terminals number 4 and 7; 5 and 8; and 6 and 9. Connected this way, each pair of coils gets 240 volts, just as it did also in the low voltage connection.

Here is the method we use to figure out the leads of a nine lead motor when they are not marked. This method is for wye connected motors only, which the vast majority of commercial motors are. Since wye connected motors get only 58% of the voltage across each coil that delta connected motors do, the motor manufacturers can use a lighter insulation, which makes the wye connected motor cheaper to build.

The first thing to do is to locate the star point. You can do this with an ohm meter. With all wires disconnected you will show continuity between three leads. There will be a fair amount of resistance, depending on the motor's horsepower rating, but only three leads should show any continuity. If you show continuity between any more leads than three, there is a short in the motor, and it needs to be re-wound. Go ahead and put line voltage across the three legs connected to the star point for a couple of seconds; the motor should turn. If you are putting more than the voltage the coils are wound for, they will probably buzz a bit, but you won't hurt the motor by doing this for only a few seconds. Motor wires are typically supposed to handle twice their intended voltage plus 1000 volts without breaking down. You can leave these wires connected to the star point, but mark them so they don't get lost while you make further tests.

Test connections for analyzing the leads of a 9 lead motor

Next, separate the remaining six wires into pairs. You should be able to get continuity in three separate pairs. These pairs will show some resistance, as did the star point; although this resistance should be about one half of what you read across the star point.

Now take one of these coils and connect one end of it to one of the wires that is part of the star circuit. (We'll call this wire number 7.) So, one end of this coil will be connected to the star circuit via wire number 7, and the other end will be left open. Now turn the power on, and test the voltage between the open end of this coil and the other two ends of the star circuit (numbers 8 and 9). This is shown in the diagram above. If you get anything but equal voltages, this is not the proper location for that coil (pair of wires). Disconnect it and try another one. On your next try, if you get equal voltages, you know you have the right coil.

Now check to see if the voltage you are reading is about 58% of line voltage; or about 150% of line voltage. If it is 58%, this means that you have the right coil, but that it is reversed. Disconnect the wire of the pair that is connected, and in its place connect the wire that formerly was unconnected. Now you should read approximately 150% of line voltage. Once you have the right coil, and the right polarity, number the wires as we show in the diagram on page 66. The wire that is directly attached to the star circuit we will call number 7; the wire that is connected to 7 will be number 4; and the other end of the coil (which is now unconnected) will be number 1. Now disconnect this coil, and start on another coil; connecting it to wire number 8.

After you get the proper coil and polarity for wire number 8, test the last remaining coil on wire number 9, and make sure you have the proper polarity. Of course, make sure you number each wire once you have it identified.

When doing these tests, run the motor as little as possible; just enough to make your tests and see rotation. Remember that sometimes you are putting twice the normal voltage on these coils; and even though they are supposed to take twice their rated voltage plus 1000 volts, you don't want to push them too far, and be sorry. Besides the problems with a higher line voltage, you have the problems of vibration, and higher than normal transient voltages.

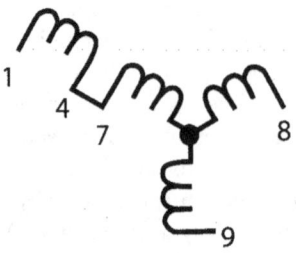

Numbering of correctly identified leads

Note that line voltage is to remain connected to wires number 7, 8, and 9 while performing all of these tests.

MISCELLANEOUS TRICKS

In this section of the book we will be covering a number of ideas covering almost all phases of electrical work. Rather than devoting a separate page to each of these items, we have decided to put them all together in one section.

When installing long runs of conduit, one of the best methods of installation is this:

Take a long chalk line and mark the run on the ceiling (or whatever surface it is you are working on) before you do anything else. Then go from one end of the run to the other and fasten your conduit hangers. (Mineralac clamps work very well for this type of installation.) After the hangers are all up, go back and install your conduit. You will find this method to work very well.

If you will be having to mount equipment on top of a concrete roof, you can get a very strong and easy mounting for your equipment by using framing channel (typically called "Unistrut" or "Kindorf").

What you do is to frame a base for the equipment to fasten to, and then nail it down to the concrete forms before the pour is made. Once the concrete is set, you will have a very sturdy place to mount your roof top equipment. Also significant is that this method makes for less roof problems, and is cheaper besides.

ROUGHING IN A BUILDING FOR DIFFERENT VOLTAGE SYSTEMS

When you are roughing-in a building that has a number of different conduit systems (120 volt power, 277 volt power, telephone conduits, fire alarm conduits, etc.), it helps a lot if you can use a few cans of spray paint and give each raceway system a separate color. It makes a major difference when you try to pull wire once the walls are closed in.

Battery terminals
If you coat any battery terminals with Anti-oxidant compound (the same stuff they use for connecting aluminum wires) you will find that it does a great job of keeping the connections corrosion free, clean, and well conducting. This is especially true for automotive batteries, but also goes for things as small as flashlights.

Moving heavy reels
If you've got a number of heavy reels of wire that you need to move around, try putting some plastic garbage bags under them, and then sliding them around; it's a lot easier than trying to "muscle" them around.

Stripping threads
If you ever strip the threads on a bolt or pipe that you really need to use, you can rill in the stripped threads with hard solder (which is a different grade of solder than regular electrical solder) and re-thread the pipe or bolt. After this, you should have no problem with the threads.

Grounding bushings

On some types of grounding bushings, instead of bringing the ground wire up to the grounding lug, and back around to the buss connection, you can do this: Simply remove the grounding lug from the body of the bushing. Then slide it over the end of the grounding conductor with the side of the lug that connects to the body of the bushing facing up. You can then screw the lug back on to the body of the bushing without much trouble. The run of the grounding conductor will now be smooth, easy, and a lot more direct. This doesn't work for all types of grounding bushings; but when it does work, it makes for a nice looking and convenient installation.

PVC conduit fittings

Misc. Tricks

If you run out of the proper types of PVC conduit fittings, you can often use a piece of PVC conduit one size larger in place of the fitting. The wall thickness of PVC is typically 1/4 inch (for the larger sizes). So if you use a conduit size that is 1/2 inch larger, it will fit very well. You can do this for a coupling, or even a 45 degree elbow. We don't recommend that you do this with a 90 degree elbow, because you are likely to scrape up the wire pretty badly as you try to pull it through the elbow. Even doing this with a 45 degree bend is a little risky. If you absolutely have to do it, make sure that you ream the inside edges of the conduit very well, leaving a smooth edge that will not cut into the wires as you pull them in.

Trim out carts

There are any number of trim out carts that you could use to make trimming out a job easier and faster. If you can build yourself a little cart mounted on wheels, that you can put a number of receptacles, plates, etc. in, and roll it around the job with you, you will find that it helps your productivity quite a bit. This eliminates most of the running around for materials that wastes so much time.

You don't have to use these carts for just the trim-out either; whenever and wherever you can effectively use them, we recommend that you do; your productivity will be better off for it. Experiment with the carts, and see what you come up with.

Setting floor boxes

Setting floor boxes to the proper height can be somewhat of a problem; here are two good methods for making sure that they are set at the correct height.

1. Many general contractors still hold to the customary procedure of making a 4 foot high mark on a column or wall. If the general contractor you are working with does this (or if you can get him to do this), you can stretch a string across the room (make sure the string is very tight, or else your measurements will be off), or use a commonly available laser level (available at www.professionalequipment.com or (800) 334-9291), and measure from the string (or laser) to the top of the box, which should be exactly 4 feet.

2. If the general contractor doesn't make the 4 foot marks for you, you can use a surveyor's tripod with a leveling instrument on it. You can then use an elevation rod to get your finish floor height. You will, though, need to get a finish floor height from somewhere else in the building.

Of course, modern advancements have helped to make this installation easier by using plastic boxes set extra high and by trimming plastic back after floor is poured. A quick and easy alternative.

Mobile Temporary Power Centers

Working with small parts

If you have to work with small parts (soldering connections to electronic components for example) you can make a pair of lineman's pliers serve as a vise by just wrapping a rubber band around the handle.

Replacing an existing panel

When you need to replace an existing circuit breaker or fuse panel (especially the larger ones with a lot of conduits feeding into them), you can save a lot of time by pulling the guts out of the" panel (so that all that is left is an empty metal can), and having a new interior custom built to the can.

By doing this you save all the time that you would spend pulling all of the conduits out of the panel, removing the panel, mounting the new panel, and feeding the old conduits into it. You also save yourself from replacing any wires that might get damaged when you try to get them out of the old panel and into the new panel. You can find someone who custom builds switchgear in almost every large city in the United States; usually they aren't a whole lot more expensive than buying from a large switchgear manufacturer through a wholesaler.

Take enough time to layout your work, and make sure that you have all the materials you will need; tools too. The better you lay out the job and prepare for it, the better your productivity will be. If you can get everything set up and ready, and then do the installation, you can do the job in a fraction of the time it would take with no preplanning.

Identifying the circuit breaker

If you have a circuit in a full circuit breaker panel that you need to identify, get a light bulb flasher and put it in a light fixture in the circuit that you are trying to identify. Then go to the panel and check the amperage readings of the hot wires with a clamp on type ammeter. When the needle in your ammeter starts to jump and fall rhythmically, you know you've got the right circuit.

Tracing a dead short

Here is a good way to trace a dead short without running back and forth to the panel:

Take the hot wire of the shorted circuit off of its fuse or circuit breaker, then wire a temporary receptacle between the fuse or circuit breaker and the wire you just removed. Plug a radio into the receptacle; it should work perfectly. Now you can start tracing the circuit; once you open the circuit you will know immediately because you will hear the radio quit.

USING MOBILE TEMPORARY POWER DISTRIBUTION CENTERS

By using temporary power centers that can be moved from one location to another, you can eliminate a lot of the knock-down and rebuilding work for future temp centers. This is especially useful for electrical contractors.

The best temporary power control that we know of is one built on a steel frame with wheels. Any type of "Unistrut", or "Kindorf" steel channel will work fine for this. On the bottom of the unit you should install the wheels, so that it is easy to move on or off the job site. Once the center is on the job site however, we recommend that you remove the wheels, and anchor the unit to the floor if at all possible. This is to prevent anyone from trying to move the temp center from one part of the site to another without having you disconnect it first. (It sounds like a crazy thing for someone to do, but rest assured that they have done a lot worse. As much as it would be purely the other guy's fault, you still don't want a dead man on your hands.)

Of course, the way you set up the wiring will depend upon what you need the temp center for an electrical contractor may want to keep several types on hand. We recommend that you use a large pull box (more properly called a cut-out box in this application) to make your connections in. Have the main feeder wires to the temp center terminate in this box; you will find this to be a good set-up for repetitive use of the temp center.

We've seen other types of temp power centers also, but all have the same basic idea: they are easily reusable. Of all the types that we've seen, we like our "Temp center on wheels" the best. It moves in and out of the job site quite easily, and because of its being constructed of strut, it is easy to build, and will be solidly grounded.

You can get all of the requirements on temporary wiring in Article 590 of the 2005 National Electrical Code.

Misc. Thoughts On Fishing Wire

TAPPING INTO A WEALTH OF INFORMATION IN TRADE MAGAZINES

Currently there are three magazines that are published nation-wide which cover the electrical construction and maintenance industry, plus several that cover the electrical wholesaling and utility markets.

Every month these magazines are published with each one having a number of very specific and informative articles. These articles give far better information and instruction to those in the industry than any technical book could. These articles are almost always written by people in the forefront of the industry and give understandable explanations of new methods, technologies, and theories.

The problem with the trade magazines is in making use of them. To save every issue can be a real problem: if you subscribe to all three magazines. this means that you will have to save thirty-six magazines per year; after five years that comes to 180 magazines. Once this point is reached you get two problems: first, finding-shelf space; and second, trying to find a single article in one of several hundred magazines (assuming that you can first remember that there was a good article written about a certain subject four or five years ago).

Here is what one fellow did to make some use of all of these articles:

He went to the office supply store and bought several boxes of sheet protectors. several three ring binders, and three hole punch. Then he went through all of his old trade magazines, and cut out every article that was of interest to him. He put the articles in the sheet dividers, and then divided them into the various notebooks by the article's subject matter.

Our friend says that he likes to use five separate notebooks: One for Engineering, one for Design, one for Motors and Controls, one for Management (his background is in contracting), and one for Lighting.

He says that he spends about an hour each month cutting out the articles that interest him and putting them in his notebooks. Then, whenever he needs some information on a specific subject, he goes to the appropriate notebook and usually finds the answers to his questions right away.

Depending on what type of work you do, you may want to arrange your own notebooks a little differently; but this is the only good method we have ever heard for getting beneficial use out of trade magazine articles.

MISCELLANEOUS THOUGHTS ON FISHING WIRE

This is a collection of various other ideas about fishing wire and cable that have come our way.

When fishing wires in overhead conduits, you can often get by without using a ladder if you take a partial length of conduit and use it as a guide to get your fish tape into the opening of the conduit. You can then push the fish tape through both the piece of conduit you are using as a guide and the conduit you want to fish wires into until the fish tape comes out at the other end. Your partner can then tie the wires onto the fish tape, and you can pull the wires as you normally do. Take care when you do this though, that you don't pull down too much. Because of your position below the conduit rather than at the same level, you will need to pull out (that is, away from the conduit opening) more than down. If you pull down, you will lose a lot of force, and perhaps damage your wires.

This is an interesting one: We heard about one fellow who was having a terrible time getting a fish tape through an underground duct. He had tried almost everything; regular fish tapes, wound fish tapes, vacuum fishing systems, etc.; but still, no results. One day he went home and found his little boy playing with one of those toy 4-wheel drive trucks. He watched as his son made this toy climb over almost anything. He watched for a while, and decided to give it a try in his underground duct.

So, he went out and bought a toy 4-wheel drive truck (he couldn't take his boy's, as you can imagine what kind of screaming that could have caused) and brought it to the job. After a few odd looks from his fellow workers, they tied a string to the back of the truck, turned it on, and put it into the end of the pipe (it was a fairly large pipe). One electrician stayed in the first manhole and fed the string into the pipe while the others went to the other end to see what would happen. After a while they heard a little bit of noise coming from the pipe; it got a little louder, and finally they saw the toy headlights coming their way.

As funny as it sounds, these little toys can really go through a lot; just about anything except a directly vertical run. Make sure though that if you have a long run you use fully charged batteries. Also make sure that you tied the string onto the toy good and tight; if for some reason the toy can't make it through, you will have to pull it back.

Trying to get a fish tape through a conduit that already has wires in it can be a very difficult proposition. Here is one method that sometimes works when nothing else will:

First off, you need a vacuum or jet line system. Then, instead of attaching a "mouse" to the end of the line, tie the line to a small plastic bag; then blow it through as you normally would. This doesn't always work, but it is better than about anything else. If you don't get good results with one plastic bag, try using two or three; sometimes that will help.

If you are trying to get a fish tape through a conduit with wires already in it; push the tape as far as you can; and then while you continue to push the fish tape, have your partner move the wires as much as he can. Exactly how much he can shake the wires will depend upon what size wires are in the pipe, and how many. Have him shake the wires as much as he can, but be careful not to damage the insulation on the wires, especlally if the wires are old.

NOTE: Whenever you push a fish tape through a conduit that already has wires in it, make very sure that the power is turned off before you start. If for some reason you absolutely cannot turn off the power, use a nylon fish tape, as they are non-conductive. If you don't have one, go out and buy one before you try to do the work; your life is worth the thirty dollars that it costs to get the right kind of tape.

If you ever have trouble pulling wires out of an old conduit, try pulling the wires one at a time, while you have another man try to shake the wire you are pulling. You can also try to pull the wire out by tying it to a car or truck of some type (in a factory a forklift will work well). Be sure first, that the conduit is very well anchored. If it is not, you may very well pull not only the wire out, but the conduit as well.

Misc. Thoughts On Fishing Wire

USING JACK CHAIN

In general, we find it much better to use a small, flexible chain (which we have always heard called "Jack Chain") than a fish tape for fishing in walls. Because of the fish tape's curve, it tends to get hung up inside of walls quite easily. The chain, on the other hand, drops straight down the void, often without ever touching the wall surface at all. It also helps to have a little bit of weight on the chain. Tying a medium sized steel nut to the end of the chain is usually more than sufficient.

USING A REVERSED LOCKNUT

Sometimes fishing a cable into an existing box can be terribly hard; it's hard enough to just get the cable in, let alone getting it into a fitting, and the fitting secured into the box.

To make this easier (without destroying your customer's walls) you should first put your fitting onto the cable before you pull it in. Next of course, you have to get the cable into the box: Sometimes it's best to pull a knock-out from the box, and have your partner drop the cable down from above; it gets a little tricky trying to get the end of the cable into the box, but if you care about your customer's walls, this is your best method. Sometimes you may have to remove a little piece of plaster or drywall just above the box, but if you can get the cable in without marring the wall, you end up with a much better job.

Last comes securing the fitting into the box. Trying to get a locknut on a cable that has been fished through a wall like this can be one of the most difficult jobs that an electrician ever has to do (for any of you fellows who have never tried to do this, it may sound simple, but we guarantee that it isn't always).

Misc. Thoughts On Fishing Wire

The locknut should be removed from the fitting before you fish the cable, and set aside. After the cable is in the box, slide the locknut over the wires, pull down on the wires to straighten the fitting in the knock-out and screw the locknut onto the fitting.

We know that sometimes this can be almost impossible; so, if you turn the locknut around, and screw it on "backwards", you will find that it is about five times easier. If you do this however, make sure that the locknut gets tightened down very well, and makes a good, strong connection. This little trick has been a real saver to the guys who do this type of work.

FISHING WIRE BY YOURSELF

Especially for small contractors, it is sometimes necessary for one man to do the job of two men and pull wires into conduit by himself. We have several little methods that will make this process a little easier.

Actually, we think that it is almost always better to have two men working together installing wires in conduit; but we also know that this can't always be done. So anyway here are some ideas on installing wire by yourself:

We've seen a man push up to 7 #12 wires into a 1/2 Inch conduit by using just a few simple techniques. First, use only solid wire whenever you can. Second, bend the ends of your wires into a smooth loop. Keep the loop fairly tight so it doesn't get too big to fit through the conduit. Thirdly, make sure that you tape up the tips of your wires. This is so that if you can't get the wires all the way through the run, there won't be any sharp edges to hang you up when you pull the wires back out. If these sharp edges are left exposed, they will catch very easily in a connector or coupling as you try to pull the wires back out of the conduit.

Some fellows say that screwing a wire nut onto the end of the wires works very well as an aid to fishing wires by yourself. We have tried this method too; and although it does help, we feel that just bending the wires works as well or better if done well. If you decide to try fishing your wires with a wire nut on the end, remember to tape up the open side of the wire nut, for the reasons that we have already mentioned.

With a little ingenuity and tenacity it is possible to fish wires by yourself that may seem almost impossible. We actually saw one electrician push the wires for a 200 amp, 3 phase, 4 wire feeder from the basement to the first floor of a nursing home — a run with two 90 degree elbows and a kick. Note that he didn't even get the aid of gravity. He

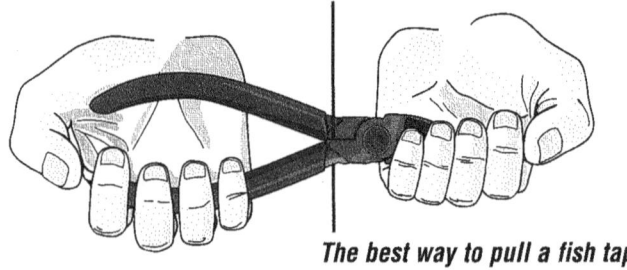

The best way to pull a fish tape

pushed it up! A real surprise was that it didn't even take him very long to get it in. So, there is a lot that you can do if you try hard enough.

If you need to fish some wires into an underfloor duct, try using a short piece of flexible conduit to sleeve the wires and fish tape as they go from the pipe to above the floor; this will make it a lot easier on your fingers; and keep the wire in better shape.

If you are pulling an underfloor run of wire and run into a difficult spot, put some type of padding on one of your shoulders (old rags, newspaper. etc.); then squat down. pull the fish tape tight over your shoulder (usually it works best to turn your back to the conduit that the wires will be coming. out of) and stand up while continuing to hold tight to the fish tape. You can get a lot more force this way than by pulling — often hundreds of pounds more.

The best way to pull a steel fish tape is shown in the illustration on page 74. By holding the tape this way. you get a firm grip on the tape without damaging it; and you also get the maximum amount of force as you can use both hands at almost your full strength.

More Fishing

MORE ON FISHING IN DIFFICULT OR IMPOSSIBLE LOCATIONS

Because fishing wires can be such a difficult project, a lot of electricians have tried to come up with easier ways to fish cable in existing buildings. In these next several pages we will explain some of the more interesting ideas that have come our way.

OVER SUSPENDED CEILINGS

We've heard several methods of installing cables over suspended ceilings. The best ones that we have heard entail the use of some type of projectile with a string tied onto it. Once the projectile and string make it to the desired location, a cable is tied onto the string, and pulled in.

One fellow we knew says he does this with a high quality sling shot; and uses a 3/8" nut as the projectile. Another electrician we talked to says he likes to use a dart gun, and tie his string onto the dart.

The most unique one we heard was about a country boy who showed up on the jobsite with his bow and arrow. He tied the string right to his arrow and let fly through the ceiling space. While it is kind of hard to argue with results, this one sounds too dangerous to us.

FINDING A FISH TAPE IN A WALL

One of the more difficult maneuvers for an electrician is to fish cable in an existing wall. Usually this requires inserting a fish tape into the wall from one end, and trying to reach into a small hole in another part of the wall and grab the fish tape.

One common method is to push one fish tape into the wall, and then use a second fish tape at the other end to try and hook the first fish tape, and pull it through easier. This usually works best if you open up the hook on at least one of the fish tapes. This can help, but still doesn't make it a lot easier; especially in walls that are insulated, which makes it very hard to tell when your partner's fish tape touches yours.

Here is one idea that has some merit: Take a 12 volt buzzer, and two 6 volt batteries. Hook up the batteries in series to get the 12 volts you will need to run your buzzer. Then connect one side of the batteries to one of the fish tapes. The other side of the battery should connect to the buzzer, and then to the other fish tape, as shown in the illustration at right. When the fish tapes touch each other the buzzer will sound; this can help sometimes, and it's not difficult to do.

Here is another idea that can be a real help: If you are fishing in a vertical wall, tie a little penlight flashlight onto the end of your fish tape. As you lower the tape into the wall space from above, your partner below will be able to see the light from the flashlight very easily; and he should have no problem grabbing it quickly. While this works sufficiently well with a fish tape, it works quite a bit better with a jack chain.

Set up for using a buzzer to help in fishing cable in concealed locations

CREDITS

Many times when we have been talking to an apprentice electrician who was having quite a time learning everything, we like to say "Look, no one is born knowing this stuff you have to learn it; if 100,000 other guys could do it, then you can too; it just takes time and effort."

Well, we weren't born knowing this stuff either, and we'd like to take a couple of pages here to thank all of the people who have taught us along the way; who also contributed many of the ideas in this book. We are very thankful to have worked with some of the best and most interesting people in the trade.

The names are listed in chronological order, more or less.

Thanks to you all.

Art Rosenwinkel, Ed Borne, Dan Ivers, Bruce Chester, Wesley House, Art Rienek, Bruce Welbourne, Gerald Cohen, Jack Kaplan, Joe Romanofski, John Biel, Leo Desmeretz, Eddy Richards, Bob Fremoux, Steve Babos, Boris Soyfer, Bogden Olejniczak, Nick Chelcun, Frank Mohap, Frank Gonzales, Randy Thomas, Richard Jaffarian, Russel Days, Jim Smith, Web Brenner, Frank Breeze, Gary Jarrell, Howard Forsythe, Same Lovelady, Alan Edelstein, Earl Lawson, Carlos Hope, C.J. Hope, Joe Tate, Jimmy Maloy, Tom Pitman, Bobby Sutton, Tom Massie, Lamar Harvell, Vick Siene, Bernie Schlaffler, Arthur Moffet, Judd Behe, Paul Smith, Ed DeEspisito, Dennis Wilfong, William Smith, Jerry Blume, Pat Santello, Jerry Gurtz, Dick Bureau, John Lindgren, Larry Maddox, and Mark Shapiro.

Our apologies if we have forgotten anybody; compiling a list like this isn't easy.

We would also like to express our thanks to the people at EC&M, ELECTRICAL CONTRACTOR, and CEE magazines who do a fine job of keeping us and everyone else in the trade abreast of current developments. A note of thanks should also go to the publishers who put out so many fine books for the electrical trade; many excellent teaching references and videos as well as the "nuts and bolts" of the electrical trade can be found at www.professionalequipment.com or by calling 800-253-0541.

Again, to all of you in the trade who have shared your expertise with us--Thank you.

NOTES

NOTES

NOTES

www.ingramcontent.com/pod-product-compliance
Lightning Source LLC
Chambersburg PA
CBHW070825250426
43671CB00036B/2151